WORLD'S GREATEST CONSPIRACY THEORIES AND SECRET SOCIETIES (2 Books in 1)

The Truth Below the Thick Veil of Deception Unearthed New World Order, Deadly Man-Made Diseases, Occult Symbolism, Illuminati, and More!

BERNADINE CHRISTNER

INTRODUCTION

Despite his stated qualms, President Barack Obama ushered in the new year on December 31, 2011, by signing the National Defense Authorization Act, which grants the government expanded powers to detain, interrogate, and punish its people. Under this new act, government agencies may order the indefinite imprisonment of American citizens without charges or trial, the possible military detention of ordinary citizens who would normally be outside of military control, and the transfer of law enforcement, penal, and custodial powers currently held by the Department of Justice to the Department of Defense. According to US Senator Lindsey Graham, a strong backer of the legislation, "the homeland is part of the battlefield" in the worldwide fight on terror.

Since the end of the Cold War and the fall of the Soviet Union in 1991, the American people have become more convinced that their government lies to them and conspires against them. Rick Ross, whose Ross Institute of New Jersey researches conspiracies, has seen that an increasing number of Americans believe that manipulative forces are at work behind the scenes of their government.

Conspiracy theorists quickly react that there are several grounds to accuse the government of shady transactions behind the scenes. While only a few whistleblowers—officially labeled "kooks and dissidents"—tried to warn the general public about secret government agencies, it was later revealed that in the late 1940s, 1950s, and 1960s, the FBI's COINTELPRO had orders to defame, disgrace, and dispose of war protesters, radical political groups, and freedom marchers by any means necessary. The CIA's evil, top-secret MK-ULTRA program did undertake heinous brainwashing and mind-altering drug experiments that may have created the Unabomber as well as the ideal assassins.

When nuclear weapons were still in their infancy in 1950, the Department of Defense exploded atomic devices in desert regions before monitoring unsuspecting citizens in cities downwind from the explosion for medical issues and fatality rates.

More than a million people were exposed to germ warfare in 1966.

Scientists from the United States Army dropped bacteria-filled light bulbs onto ventilation grates in the New York City subway system.

Senate hearings in 1977 showed that 239 densely populated locations, including San Francisco, Washington, D.C., Key West, Panama City, Minneapolis, and St. Louis, had been polluted with biological agents between 1949 and 1969.

Evidence emerged in 1995 indicating the biological weapons used during the Gulf War were developed in Houston and Boca Raton and tested on Texas Department of Corrections inmates.

In the years after the World Trade Center was destroyed on September 11, 2001, Mike Ward of PopMatters (January 3, 2003) has described "probably the most astounding explosion of 'conspiracy theories in American history." Angry conjecture, centered mostly on dirty government deals, ulterior objectives, and suspected cooperation in the assaults, has reached a pitch that easily surpasses that which followed the Kennedy assassination."

Conspiracy theories are often riddled with internal contradictions, and normal people reject some as absolutely bizarre and insane.

Often, the truth is somewhere in the center, and the role of the diligent researcher is to make an informed decision. Unfortunately, those who want to dominate and influence others may get the final laugh if certain conspiracy theories are dismissed as too wild and outlandish to merit consideration.

Conspiracy theorists fear that Big Brother's eyes and ears are getting more active throughout the country.

Cameras are appearing on street corners around the United States and other nations such as England. They are ostensibly there to assist police in scanning license plates on stolen cars, apprehending thieves, and escaping killers. In addition, many cameras have facial recognition capabilities and can cross-reference any citizen suspected of antisocial behavior or even the most minor offenses with an extensive database.

Radio Frequency Identification (RFID) chips the size of a grain of sand is used to track children's attendance and movements at school, retail product sales trends, and manufacturing worker habits. According to reports, plans are to implant a chip in all United States and European infants.

Government agents may readily monitor both landlines and mobile phones.

An anachronism is making a private call. The FBI has been compelled to disclose that it routinely monitors Internet radio talk shows throughout the United States, as well as email and internet surfing habits.

Even the average American citizen, who is more interested in sports and paying the bills than politics and conspiracies, may be uneasy about the fact that the National Defense Authorization Act has expanded the Patriot Act's power and that three Republican presidential candidates openly support water-boarding as a tool of interrogation. How far would the government go in using its new powers to force a person accused of treason or terrorism to plead to those charges?

From its inception, America has been a breeding ground for conspiracies and secret groups. For example, Christopher Columbus had apocalyptic views, claiming to have gotten a vision that the world will end in 1650 and that it was his divine purpose to locate a new continent that would be the site of the new heaven and new earth prophesied by St. John in the Book of Revelation. In the 1600s, the master Freemason Sir Francis Bacon thought America was the New Atlantis, bringing out a New World Order that would return all humans to the earthly paradise during the Golden Age.

Petty conspiracies about political or corporate competitors are as ancient as the human brain, writes Daniel Pipes in Front-Page magazine (January 13, 2004). However, worries of vast conspiracies, such as a secret organization plotting to take over the globe, date back barely 900 years and have "been operational for barely two centuries, since the French Revolution." While Madame Guillotine was shaving royal heads, some residents blamed the revolution on the Bavarian Illuminati's political machinations and its grip on the Jacobins.

Fear of such conspiracies and mysterious groups has filled American history with warnings of hidden machinations by Freemasons, Zionists, Roman Catholics, Communists, World Bankers,

Bilderbergers, Illuminati, Secret Government, New Agers, and alien invasions. Conspiracy theories have evolved into self-fulfilling histories of nefarious intrigues responsible for the killings of Abraham Lincoln, James Garfield, John F. Kennedy, Robert F. Kennedy, Martin Luther King, Jr., Malcolm X, and Princess Diana.

Diana, Princess of Wales According to polls, a growing proportion of Americans feel they have not been given the truth about Pearl Harbor, the Gulf of Tonkin, the Oklahoma City bombing, the Waco fires, or the 9/11 Twin Towers.

Sometimes it seems like these paranoid folks are on to something. When conspiracies like the ones mentioned above prove to be real or partly correct, the assumption that there is a kernel of truth in even the most outlandish conspiracy theory seems to be true as well. Michael Barkun, a political scientist at Syracuse University and the author of A Culture of Conspiracy: Apocalyptic Visions in Contemporary America (2003), thinks that every conspiracy theory has three principles: Nothing occurs by chance; nothing is as it seems; everything is interconnected. According to Barkun, the heart of conspiracy theories "lies in efforts to distinguish and explain evil." Barkun also claims that current conspiracy theories have undergone significant new development, incorporating the occult, heretical, and unfashionable, such as spiritualism, alchemy, and theosophy.

With the advent of the Internet, anybody can become a conspiracy theorist and broadcast unregulated, uncontested, and uncontested accusations of government corruption, racial propaganda, or extraterrestrial abduction throughout the globe. There are hundreds of active websites devoted to conspiracy theories and secret organizations on Google alone. Sharing tales about conspiracies and secret organizations is similar to spreading nasty gossip. It is necessary to know what is factual and what is just a mirror of someone else's particular biases and views.

For many years, we have investigated and examined the immense effect of conspiracy theories on society and how people's views may be swayed for good or ill via the spread of specific ideas, theories, and beliefs. While this book seems to capture the more gloomy faces of human history, the pictures that emerge in the dark mirrors reflecting depictions of turmoil, confusion, and deception down through the years, we have done our best to approach this work objectively. We do not believe in any conspiracy theories and do not belong to any secret societies. It is up to the reader to choose if this book is a work of amusement or enlightenment, a word of astonishment or a word of warning.

AIDS/HIV

According to conspiracy theorists, AIDS did not originate in Africa but rather in secret government labs that developed this and other heinous biological weapons.

The first African woman to win the Nobel Peace Prize, Kenyan environmentalist Wangari Maathai, utilized the world spotlight to assert that the AIDS virus was an intentionally designed biological weapon used in warfare. She rejected the hypothesis that AIDS (acquired immunodeficiency syndrome) originated in monkeys, pointing out that Africans had lived near monkeys from time immemorial. But, she noted, there was no denying the sobering truth that 25 million of the 38 million people who have AIDS worldwide are Africans, with the vast majority being women.

Women make up the majority of afflicted Africans.

The United States State Department welcomed Maathai on her Nobel Peace Prize triumph but disagreed with her statements that the human immunodeficiency virus (HIV) that causes AIDS was created as a bioweapon in a Western laboratory for the goal of mass extinction. While such a statement may be expected from the State Department, conspiracy theorists are quick to point out that one of the primary goals of the New World Order and its agents working in the shadows behind every government in the world is to reduce the number of people in power. Substantially increase the world's population

Dr. Robert Gallo of the National Cancer Institute and Luc

Montagnier of the Pasteur Institute in Paris claimed to have discovered the AIDS virus in 1984. A lawsuit was filed in 1987 to resolve the dispute. However, the virus's discoverers have never agreed on the virus's origins or the genesis of AIDS. Montagnier thought that the virus's origins were unknown and critical to differentiate between the virus's beginnings and the AIDS pandemic. Gallo, the more powerful of the two experts, claimed that the virus descended from a common viral parent seen in animals and was transmitted to humans via monkeys. Gallo said that in 1983, a year before he found the virus, Ann Giudici Fettner, a freelance writer who had lived in Africa, informed him that green monkeys in central Africa caused AIDS. However, in her book The Truth about AIDS, Fettner never mentions green monkeys and stresses her belief that AIDS started in America. Despite the lack of scientific studies to back up Gallo's green monkey thesis, the explanation remained popular among the media and the general public until the late 1990s, when another group of American scientists claimed to have uncovered the virus's origin in a kind of chimp.

Many conspiracy theorists have never accepted the "out of Africa" and green monkey, chimp, or goat theory for the origin of AIDS. The first homosexual males were diagnosed with "immunodeficiency disease" in 1979. During the first year of the pandemic, the victims were all young, mostly white, previously healthy, highly educated, and promiscuous—and they all resided in Manhattan. By 1980, the illness had spread to homosexual males in San Francisco, Los Angeles, Denver, St. Louis, and Chicago. In June 1981, an official AIDS pandemic was announced. Before this period, AIDS was unknown in Africa, and the pandemic did not begin there until late 1982. Gallo became world-famous for discovering the green monkeys in Africa, harboring the sickness for generations before the pandemic in 1984.

However, a perplexing time issue has arisen. If the first cases of AIDS were reported to the Centers for Disease Control (CDC) in 1979, are we to think that all of the homosexual males in Manhattan who caught the disease had just been to Africa and been bitten by green monkeys? Or is there a link between government-sponsored hepatitis B studies that started with homosexual males in Manhattan in 1978, the year before?

The HIV pandemic that erupted in 1979? In 1980, the government funded comparable hepatitis B studies in San Francisco, Los Angeles, Denver, St. Louis, and Chicago. The experimental vaccination put into all of those homosexual guys was said to have been created on chimps.

Early in the 1970s, stories began to circulate about covert government biowarfare research and scientists undertaking "species-jumping" operations, including mixing viruses and planting them into animal and human cell cultures. President Richard Nixon merged the United States Army's biowarfare division at Fort Detrick, Maryland, with the National Cancer Institute in 1971. Although the initiative was promoted to the public as part of the president's "War on Cancer," it also linked the army's DNA and genetic engineering operations with anticancer research and molecular biology studies. Furthermore, cancer research programs undertaken by commercial firms were integrated into anticancer research efforts performed by the CIA, the Centers for Disease Control and Prevention, and the World Health Organization. As research advanced, hundreds of novel laboratory hybrids, recombinant and mutant viruses were developed. A few socially conscious scientists started to warn others that some newly developed viruses may be exceedingly harmful if released from the laboratory. Finally, due to the efforts of a few whistleblowers, news spread that government scientists had created a synthetic biological agent that did not exist naturally and against which no natural immunity could be established.

Knowledge of what had been accomplished traveled quickly to other government researchers all across the globe. The Danish doctor Johannes Clemmesen warned in 1973 that the transmissibility of such genetically engineered viral agents may unleash a global cancer outbreak if they ever escaped the laboratory. Then, in 1979, his foreboding forecast came true with the onset of AIDS among Manhattan's homosexual community.

Although most people accept Robert Gallo's explanation that the AIDS pandemic is the consequence of a monkey virus crossing species, conspiracy theorists have produced their theories about AIDS/HIV. Some of the more persistent hypotheses are as follows:

- The River: A Journey to the Source of HIV-AIDS, by Edward Hopper, pushes the notion that HIV arose from SIV (simian immunodeficiency virus), present in chimps. Hooper describes a scenario in which the villain is Dr. Hilary Koprowski, a virologist working for Wistar in Philadelphia.

- In the early 1950s, the Research Institute utilized a hurriedly brewed chimp kidney culture to create a million doses of an oral vaccine for a huge experimental polio immunization campaign in the Belgian Congo. The pharmaceutical firm placing pressure on Koprowski to beat Dr. Salk and Dr. Sabin to the market with the first commercially accessible polio vaccine fueled his hurry and speed in executing the mass immunization.

- In the 1970s, the World Health Organization, controlled by the New World Order, purposefully administered tainted vaccinations to individuals in third-world nations, causing the AIDS pandemic. Africa was originally targeted in a smallpox eradication operation so that a connection could later be drawn that AIDS began in Africa.

- Around 1977, US military scientists at Fort Detrick bioengineered HIV by fusing the Visna and HTLV viruses. It was tested on convicts who willingly agreed to be injected with the virus in return for an early release. The virus spread from these freed criminals to a larger population, particularly the LGBT community.

- The Soviet KGB produced the viruses and circulated misinformation suggesting the CIA was behind the disease's spread.

- AIDS was developed as a result of biowarfare research done by the United States government with the explicit goal of removing surplus population among blacks, homosexuals, and other social groups.

- Dr. Alan Cantwell (AIDS and the Doctors of Death: An Inquiry into the Origins of the AIDS Epidemic and Queer Blood: The Secret AIDS Genocide Plot) believes that HIV is a genetically modified virus that was introduced into the gay and bisexual population by the US government scientists between 1978 and 1981 in Manhattan, Los Angeles, St.

Louis, Denver, and Chicago under the guise of hepatitis B experiments.

- Dr. Gary Glum (Full Disclosure) alleges that he was given top-secret information that the AIDS virus was produced at Cold Spring Harbor Laboratory in Cold Spring Harbor, New York. The World Health Organization and the Red Cross are participating in the plot to spread AIDS, issued in 1978 as part of the Illuminati's and the New World Order's broader population-control scheme. Glum cautions that the virus is significantly more readily transferred than medical records suggest and that it may be transferred via kissing, mosquito bites, and casual contact. Dr. Glum further claims that Upjohn Pharmaceuticals possesses various medicinal remedies for AIDS but that the government has prohibited drug release.

- The Nation of Islam and the New Black Panther Party, led by Louis Farrakhan, have accused Jewish physicians of inventing AIDS to exterminate black people across the globe.

- Dr. Leonard G. Horowitz (Emerging Viruses: AIDS and Ebola—Nature, Accident, or Intentional? and Death in the Air: Globalism, Terrorism, and Toxic Warfare) theorizes that AIDS was engineered by US government defense contractors such as Litton Bionetics to target Jews, blacks, and Hispanics as the first to be eliminated in a massive population-control program.

WOODPECKER

The covert Russian "woodpecker" tap-tap-tap blasted ELF at U.S. coastal communities, triggering panic, sadness, and suicides among the inhabitants.

Warnings that Soviet submarines were beaming ELF at US coastal towns alarmed conspiracy theorists in 1975 and the years that followed. (ELF, or extremely low frequency, refers to the radio frequency range of 3 to 300 Hz.) Conspiracy theorists claim that the low frequency caused widespread illness, migraines, depression, and even suicides among the coastal population. Listening equipment picked up the ELF signal, which was characterized as a "tap, tap, tap, tap, tap" sounded very much like a woodpecker banging on a tree.

A secret Russian neuro medical study showed that each mood, idea, or emotion that people experience has its own set of brain frequencies. Russian scientists and psychologists produced a comprehensive list of these brain processes with their specific frequency. The submarines might shoot ELF waves for wrath, suicide, hysteria, desire, psychosis, or despair at hundreds, if not thousands, of unwitting victims from the murky seas of the United States coast. The Soviet submarines were not attempting to eradicate the whole country. If they could create neurological breakdowns in coastal dwellers, it would be proof that the human brain can be manipulated, even at a distance, by using ELF conveyed by pulse-modulated microbeams. Eugene, Oregon, USA

One of the cities where the Soviets' pulsating "woodpecker" ELF pulses at crucial brain-wave rhythms significantly impacted.

It was well known that the United States Navy utilized ELF to communicate with underwater submarines. Because of the electrical conductivity of saltwater, most electromagnetic signals are inhibited from reaching undersea vehicles. ELF is rarely utilized in everyday communications because its very low transmission rate necessitates installing a very big antenna spanning several kilometers.

According to conspiracy theorists, US military scientists started to understand that the "woodpecker" was more than just cold war hysteria. The navy finally committed more than $25 million on ELF research. It wasn't long before America had its fleet of "woodpeckers" roaming the coastline of Soviet-bloc countries.

Senator Gaylord Nelson of the United States later pushed the navy to release their studies proving that ELF broadcasts may change human blood chemistry. Dr. Susan Bawin and Dr. W. Ross Adey demonstrated in 1976 that ELF fields impact nerve cells.

The unusual anomalous sky glows, strange lightning, and mysterious plasma phenomena were seen in the skies surrounding the woodpecker transmitter sites in the USSR in the summer of 1977. According to the Washington Post (September 23, 1977), a "strange, star-like ball of light" was spotted in the sky above Petrozavodsk, Soviet Karelia, "spreading like a jellyfish and pouring down shafts of light."

The United States government built and maintained two locations in Wisconsin's Chequamegon National Forest and Michigan's Escanaba State Forest, each employing power lines as antennas extending fourteen to twenty-eight miles in length. Ecologists grew worried about environmental conditions and human health issues caused by the large quantities of energy produced and released by

ELF. In 1984 a federal court ordered development to be paused until more research could be conducted and reviewed.

During the massive floods that drenched the Midwest in 1993, many saw "strange bursts of light" that poured from "the tops of storm clouds into the upper sky." According to the Kansas City Star, the strange bursts of light resembled "jellyfish." On September 24, 1993, the newspaper stated that the light flashes were "brightest where they peak out—typically about 40 miles high—so you have the jellyfish body at the top with tentacles trailing down."

The antennas of the Chequamegon and Escanaba ELF sites were ordered decommissioned in 2004. According to conspiracy theorists, it makes no difference if the government demolishes the two sites. HAARP greatly outperforms those pesky Russian and American woodpeckers in terms of weather control and global military dominance.

AUM SHINRIKYO (SUPREME TRUTH)

Asahara Shoko helped bring his apocalyptic prophesies to fruition by having his followers unleash sarin nerve gas in Tokyo subway stations.

Asahara Shoko (born Chizuo Matsumoto) founded Aum Shinrikyo, a cult with hundreds of followers, in 1987. Shoko/Matsu moto claimed to have attained enlightenment when alone in India's Himalaya Mountains in 1986. He was given the holy name Asahara Shoko, a new religion named Aum (Sanskrit for the forces of destruction and creation), Shinrikyo (teaching of the highest truth), and a mission to teach the truth about the universe's creation and destruction. Furthermore, Aum's excellent efforts would prevent the Apocalypse from occurring. Following considerable opposition, the In Japan, the organization was recognized as a religious body.

Asahara Shoko was heavily inspired by the Christian Bible's book of Revelation, Nostradamus' prophesies, Tibetan Buddhist teachings on transmigration, and different Hindu themes and deities. Aum's principal deity is Shiva, the Hindu god of devastation. Initially, Asahara instructed his disciples to endeavor to turn bad energy into good energy. To escape the devastation of nuclear war, thirty thousand students must experience real spiritual emancipation via his teachings.

Few outsiders realized Asahara had a grand plot to take over Japan and, ultimately, the globe. Shinto (Supreme Truth Party), a new political party founded by Aum, ran twenty-five candidates in the 1990 Japanese legislative election. If all twenty-five Shinrito candidates had not been defeated at the election, things may have been different. Instead, Asahara started to get apocalyptic visions emphasizing the impending end of the planet. One of the terrifying prophecies from the spirit realm predicted that the United States would ignite World War III with Japan, ushering in Armageddon. Asahara urged his supporters that they needed to move quickly to grab control of Japan with such a disaster looming. One of the Aum belief system's tenets believed that followers might alleviate negative karma by undergoing different types of hardship. Indeed, it seemed natural that nonbelievers may be helped in erasing their negative karma if Aum could aid them in their suffering—even death.

Aum caused a series of strange chemical incidents in Japan in 1994. Sarin nerve gas clouds killed seven people and wounded hundreds more in central Japan's Kita-Fukashi area. On March 20, 1995, during morning rush hour in Tokyo, ten high-ranking Aum adherents boarded five subway trains at separate stations and unleashed sarin at a preset time, killing twelve people and wounding thousands more. Tokyo police investigated the cult and discovered that between October 1988 and March 1995, Asahara might have ordered the death of thirty-three Aum members who defied his directives or wanted to quit the cult. In May 1995, Japanese authorities arrested Asahara and 104 of his followers.

In October 1995, the Japanese government removed its recognition of the Aum as a religious organization. Still, in 1997, a government panel opted not to apply the country's Anti-Subversive Law against the group, which would have banned the cult. However, due to worries that the Aum would commit future terrorist acts, legislation passed in 1999 authorized the government to maintain police monitoring of the organization. In July 2001, Russian officials apprehended a group of Russian Aum supporters who intended to detonate explosives near Tokyo's Imperial Palace to liberate Asahara and transfer him to Russia.

Aum changed its name to Aleph ("to begin again") in January 2000, under the leadership of Fumihiro Joyu, and claimed to have repudiated the violent and cult-like practices of Aum.

Its founder's apocalyptic doctrines, However, in early 2005, Japanese authorities raided four cult-related locations. Inside one, they discovered a Geiger detector and a largely built concrete bunker two levels deep. Many worried Japanese wondered whether the location was intended to take over the complex facilities near Mount Fuji where Aum Shinrikyo formerly produced sarin gas and tortured and cremated wayward members.

LOUIS BEAM

Louis Beam became a lone wolf terrorist against the government, which he saw as betraying the white race.

Louis Beam (1946–), one of the extreme right's most powerful and explosive figures, is often regarded as the first significant practitioner of the "lone-wolf" or "leaderless resistance" type of activity. Beam initially started involved as a Klansman, then as a neo-Nazi with Christian Identity links. For more than three decades, he has waged an aggressive campaign against a government that he considers corrupt.

Despotic and under the direction of a multinational Jewish conspiracy

Beam grew up in Lake Jackson, Texas, amid the segregated South. Following an eighteen-month term of service in Vietnam, he returned to Texas in 1968 and joined the Texas chapter of the United Klans of America (UKA), led by Texas grand dragon Frank Converse.

Beam left the UKA in 1976 to join David Duke's Knights of the Ku Klux Klan (KKK), where he was assigned to train Klansmen in guerilla warfare.

Beam became more concerned about the white supremacist movement's dwindling membership rolls, and it became his personal goal to revitalize the Klan somehow. During 1978 and 1979, he recruited Klan members among US Army soldiers at Fort Hood in Texas, and by 1980, Duke had elevated him to the grand dragon of the Texas KKK.

Beam sparked major tensions between refugee Vietnamese shrimp workers and local fishers who shared Gulf Coast waters in the Galveston Bay region of Texas in 1981. The war cry was "White Power! We Will Fight!" Beam sent in armed Klansmen to defend the Texas fisherman while harassing refugee fishers and other Vietnamese families in the vicinity.

In collaboration with the Southern Poverty Law Center, the Vietnamese Fishermen's Association filed an injunction to stop the Klan's harassment. A U.S. district judge decided in favor of the plaintiffs in May 1981, ordering Beam and his men to stop participating in illegal acts of violence and intimidation.

Beam stepped down as Texas grand dragon to become an ambassador for Richard Butler's Aryan Nations. While residing at the Aryan headquarters in Hayden Lake, Idaho, the beam created a complex computer network to disseminate racist and anti-Semitic propaganda more efficiently. Beam also devised the infamous assassination "point system," which assigned points to would-be assassins depending on the value of their targets. When the sick Butler chose to stand down, all signs were that Beam would take over as head of the Aryan Nations.

Beam and thirteen others were indicted by a federal grand jury in Fort Smith, Arkansas, on April 24, 1987, on charges that included firebombing a Jewish community center in Bloomington, Indiana, attempting to blow up a natural gas pipeline in Fulton, Arkansas, purchasing firearms and explosives in Missouri and Oklahoma, and stealing over $4 million from banks and armored vehicles.

In Washington State, Beam fled to Mexico using the code name "Lonestar" before the indictment was released. The beam was apprehended and handed over to US investigators on November 6, 1987, after an altercation with Mexican federal judicial police in Guadalajara that left one officer gravely injured.

Beam elected to defend himself in court with the help of Kirk Lyons, a lawyer renowned for sympathizing with radical-right clients. After seven weeks of testimony and twenty hours of deliberation, the jury acquitted Beam and his co-defendants on all counts on April 7, 1988, inflicting a significant defeat to the federal government's effort to police the extreme right throughout the 1980s.

Beam hailed the establishment of the "Fresh Right," a movement that coupled Christian Identity to "the formation of a national state for the white man, an Aryan republic inside the confines of the existing occupied country," filled with new confidence in his cause and disdain toward the federal government. Simultaneously, Beam connected America's extreme right to "freedom movements" in Syria, Libya, Iran, and Palestine. Palestinian leader Yasser Arafat, in Beam's opinion, was a particularly admirable character.

The beam was widely regarded as one of the most important personalities in American radicalism during the first half of the 199However, he. He gradually fell out of favor with the movement's extremists because he prioritized purging the country of the sins of the federal government above anti-Semitism. The beam was also heard making anti-Nazi remarks.

Beam indicated in an October 1996 letter to supporters that it had been ten years since his arrest, trial, and eventual release at Fort Smith, Arkansas. He'd given the cause ten more years, and now he planned to devote his family the rest of his life. Furthermore, he confessed for the first time that he had been exposed to Agent Orange while serving in Vietnam and that his health was deteriorating.

Beam now concentrates his energies exclusively on his website.

BIG BROTHER

According to conspiracy theorists, the warning is no longer a literary allusion—Big Brother is monitoring us.

The classic novel 1984 depicts a bleak future in which a totalitarian government known as "the Party" maintains full control over its citizens at all times. Many consider this work to be an almost perfect prophetic vision of an extremely grim and terrible future by George Orwell, one that seems to be actual unfolding right before our eyes in the twenty-first century

We now can rule and monitor all people via brainwashing tactics, media (including television, movies, and computer-like gadgets that emit propaganda), tracking and espionage systems that follow our every move, and even the capacity to see and hear through walls. However, most of these items did not exist in 1949, when Orwell wrote about them.

In Orwell's book, "Big Brother," the supreme leader of the Party has become associated with a totalitarian society in which businesses and the government take away our freedom, privacy, and capacity to think for ourselves, governing over us with unlimited power and control. The Party's motto, "Big Brother Is Watching You," is constantly aired in and via all media in the book. There is nowhere to hide since banners, posters, movie and television displays, laptops, stamps, and so on are everywhere.

Coins, even idea transmission, all communicate Big Brother's proclamation of full dominance. By extension, the terms Big Brother and "Big Brother Is Watching You" have become ubiquitous in referring to any conspiracies engaged in bringing about a One World Government.

MAE BRUSSELL

Years of in-depth investigation persuaded Mae Brussell that the Kennedy murder, the CIA, and Nazi Germany were part of a global network of secret organizations.

Mae Brussell became renowned to her many followers as the radio queen after seventeen years of feisty and fiery radio broadcasts. She warned her listeners that a shadow government covertly governed the United States.

Conspiracy theorists are those who believe in conspiracies.

Mae Magnin was born in Beverly Hills in 1922, the daughter of famous Wilshire Boulevard Temple Rabbi Edgar Magnin and the great-granddaughter of Isaac Magnin, founder of I. Magnin apparel businesses. Mae was married with five children and lived in Southern California in 1963. She grew persuaded that Lee Harvey Oswald could not have carried out the John F. Kennedy assassination.

As a result of her involvement in killing John F. Kennedy as a lone wolf, her interests shifted from being a housewife and mother to searching for clues to the Kennedy and Oswald killings and becoming a conspiracy theorist. Mae bought the twenty-six-volume Warren Commission report on the murders and started reading, filing, and cross-referencing material from a broad range of books, journals, and official records.

After years of rigorous investigation, Mae determined that the Kennedy assassination showed linkages to the CIA and Nazi Germany and a wide range of modern and historical organizations and events across the globe. It seemed to her that the international network of secret organizations and conspiracies that had formed and purportedly defeated the Axis forces during World War II had gone underground and very successfully continued their mission to dominate governments worldwide. Mae recognized many of the same names and deceptive strategies to convert Germany from a sophisticated and scientific country in the 1920s and 1930s into a savage and cruel machine of bigotry and hate in document after document.

Mae was asked to speak as a guest on KLRB, a local FM radio station, in June 1971, after seven years of study, to express her opinions on political killings. The reaction from the crowd was positive, and she soon had her show.

Dialogue: Conspiracy, show (later changed to World Watchers International). Mae provided the material from her raw data files with her audience almost every week for seventeen years, covering everything from the president's death in Dallas to the Iran-Contra investigations to what she called the Reagan administration's atrocities and high crimes.

When Mae's program did not have a host station, she taped her broadcasts at home on a little cassette tape recorder and sent them to a list of subscribers. Her radio show was taken up by KAZU in Pacific Grove, California, in 1983, but she was pulled off the air in 1988 due to death threats. Until June 13, 1988, she continued to send out recordings explaining her study and discoveries. On October 3, 1988, Mae Brussell died of cancer. Her art may be seen at http://www.maebrussell.com.

X-FILES

The X-Files was the definitive series of the 1990s for conspiracy theorists, UFO enthusiasts, and paranormal fans.

In 1993, Chris Carter, creator of the Fox network's television series The X-Files, crafted a blend of UFO mythology, growing public distrust of the government, and growing interest in the paranormal that, over its nine-year run, usually finished as the second-most-popular drama (after ER on NBC) among young adults. The X-Files had an estimated 20 million viewers per episode during its peak season in 1997. Sandy Grushow, the head of Fox Entertainment, said in 2002, just before the series' last episode, that The

The X-Files had earned the firm more than $1 Billion.

The X-Files was, without a doubt, the defining series of the 1990s for conspiracy theorists and paranormal enthusiasts. But, rather than becoming a cult sensation enjoyed by the political fringe, the series defied all expectations and filled the general audience with paranoia. Fox Mulder (David Duchovny) and Dana Scully (Gillian Anderson) of the FBI followed UFOs, extraterrestrial bounty hunters, and bad government officials regularly, declaring to their viewers that "the truth is out there." However, since an ultrasecret and brutal government organization hid the truth, they had to "trust no one." And all it took was watching the news or reading the daily newspaper to see real-life, high-level cover-ups or acquire a skepticism of the government after high-handed errors like Iran-Contra, Watergate, Ruby Ridge, and Waco.

The X-Files won the Golden Globes for best television drama, best actor in a television drama (Duchovny), and best actress in a television drama (Anderson) in 1996.

According to Carter's mythology for the series, the alien invasion began in ancient times. It was uncovered in 1947 by the United States military and a secret section of the government after a flying saucer crash at Roswell, New Mexico. Although Mulder and Scully investigated vampires, ghosts, and a wide range of monsters, it was the complicated, sometimes downright confusing, UFO mythology that held the series together and kept fans returning week after week to track the agents' progress in cracking the ultimate case that would force the secret government to admit the truth about aliens.

On June 19, 1998, the X-Files motion feature Fight the Future was released, bringing the TV show's small-screen fear to big-screen theatres throughout the country. The picture topped the box office revenues in its first week, making $31 million. It has subsequently earned more than $100 million.

The last two seasons of The X Files featured less of Mulder, who was purportedly hiding from the secret government, and less participation from Scully, who appeared to have graduated to a type of advising role. Instead, the show's new costars, Robert Patrick as Agent John Doggett and Annabeth Gish as Agent Monica Reyes, took up most tasks to track down monsters, restless spirits, and wayward aliens.

Before the series finished in May 2002, Scully and Mulder had been kidnapped, and Scully, who had previously been deemed unable to have children, had given birth under inexplicable circumstances. Scully's child, William, was Mulder's by donor sperm or by the extraterrestrials artificially inseminating her with her partner's seed during one of their abduction episodes, even though loyal fans of the series were denied witnessing Scully-Mulder weddings or even a discreet love scene between the two. Or maybe Chris Carter did not want to show us everything. The story ended with the two soul mates fleeing the continual threat of the Cigarette Smoking Man and bounty-hunting aliens to start a new life together.

The X-Files, often lauded as a cultural phenomenon and often regarded as the most successful science-fiction series in television history up to that point, had an immeasurable impact on the public's ideas about UFOs, abductions, and government conspiracies.

THE AMERICAN FAMILY ASSOCIATION

According to the American Family Association, television is a "garbage land" and a wide wasteland.

Rev. Donald Wildmon founded the National Federation for Decency in 1977, and it was renamed the American Family Association (AFA) in 1988. Wildmon, a former Methodist clergyman, has made a name for himself as a powerful force in banning trashy and unpleasant television commercials. During the Reagan administration, Wildmon was appointed to Attorney General Edwin Meese's Commission on Pornography by the commission's executive director, Alan Sears, and managed to convince seventeen thousand convenience shops to remove publications like Playboy and Penthouse off their shelves. Tim Wildmon, Donald Wildmon's son, took over the President of the AFA in 2005, controlling a 200-station radio network and a monthly magazine sent to roughly 200,000 people subscribers, as well as around a hundred workers

The American Family Association's Position

- A burgeoning LGBT media presence is changing the United States into a skewed society.

- Prominent LGBT leaders have openly supported the legalization of pedophilia, incest, sadomasochism, and bestiality.

- Homosexuality must be condemned with the same zeal as murder, thievery, and adultery.

- Homosexuals were the primary architects of Nazism and Nazi horrors. Satanism and homosexuality are extensively promoted by Procter & Gamble.

Activities: Through its radio stations, pamphlets, and monthly magazine, the AFA has persuaded hundreds of thousands of people to boycott national marketers that promote items or notions that it finds objectionable.

THE AIRSHIP OF 1897

Members of a secret group in communication with extraterrestrials sailed a gigantic airship, typically described as resembling a cone-shaped riverboat, over the Atlantic Ocean in 1897, years before any known terrestrial agency had managed heavier-than-air flight.

The United States, and subsequently the rest of the globe.

The globe was poised firmly on the verge of the twentieth century in 1897. Karl Benz and Henry Ford produced their first four-wheeled vehicles in 1893. In 1895, Auguste and Louis Lumière produced the cinematograph, Guglielmo Marconi established radiotelegraphy, and Konstantin Tsiolkovsky developed the rocket reaction theory Propulsion.

In 1897, the Royal Automobile Club was created in London, and automobiles on the road were becoming quicker by the year. However, no heavier-than-air vehicles were racing over the sky, and several bright experts proclaimed that such flying aircraft were aerodynamically impossible to make.

Nonetheless, on April 7, 1897, residents of Wesley, Iowa, saw a cone-shaped airship with brilliantly lighted windows in its side. Unfortunately, witnesses were unable to establish how it was pushed or what kept it aloft.

The airship landed two miles north of Springfield, Illinois, on April 15. The occupants of the ship indicated that they had landed to repair their electrical equipment and searchlight equipment.

The airship returned to Iowa on April 17 and landed near Waterloo.

One of the inmates brandished a weapon to keep curious at a safe distance from the machine. Journal journalists reported the airship as being around forty feet long and built like a gigantic cigar, with winglike extensions on the sides and a steering system at the back. A dome on the machine's roof topped it off.

The airship barnstormed Arkansas and Texas on April 21 and 22. It woke up a former senator in Harrisburg, Arkansas, around midnight. Members of the flying crew told him that the craft's designer was a great genius from St. Louis who had found the key of suspending gravity's rules. The airship had taken nineteen years to develop, but since it was not yet complete, the crew chose to cruise at night. They planned to place the airship on public display after completing a successful mission to Mars.

A renowned Texas farmer was awoken at midnight on April 24 by a peculiar whirring sound and the bright lights of what he thought were angels in a heavenly vehicle. Instead, the visitors told him that they did not come from heaven.

But from a little hamlet in Iowa, where five of these airships had been built. The craft was made of a newly found substance that could sustain itself in the air. The driving force was highly concentrated electricity.

Landing and contact reports poured in from throughout the country during the next several weeks. Sightings were recorded from all around the globe during the summer months of 1897. Strange airborne objects were reported above Sweden and Norway in July and August. On the same day, what looked to be the same flying object was seen off the coast of Norway and above Vancouver, British Columbia.

Count von Zeppelin revealed an airship in 1898, but the early versions had such a limited flying range that successful trips from Germany to England were impossible. Orville and Wilbur Wright achieved the first flight with a heavier-than-air vehicle in 1903, with a plane that stayed aloft for twelve seconds and traveled 120 feet. However, no terrestrial organization had built an aerial vehicle capable of traversing the world at the speed and ease of the airship flown by the unknown inventors from Iowa or St. Louis in 1897. As a result, many academics assume that the builders of the 1897 airship were members of a secret organization, maybe one that had been in contact with alien intelligence—or their records and artifacts—for thousands of years.

Numerous European occult organizations have been formed around the concept that a secret society acquired a high degree of scientific knowledge centuries ago and has carefully concealed this hazardous information from the rest of humankind ever since. A recurring motif is that selected brilliant persons in ancient Egypt and Persia were granted access to the world's sophisticated technology archives. Many hundreds of years ago, these ancient masters learned to replicate many of the accomplishments of the Titans of Atlantis—and drew the notice of extraterrestrials who had been watching Earth for evidence of high intellect.

The choice to build a society inside a society may have reflected the members' highly developed moral sense and their realization of the enormous responsibility that holding this old knowledge entails. They may have opted to stay quiet until the rest of the world grew educated enough to cope intelligently with such a high level of technological achievement. However, now and again, the secret organization may decide that the moment has come to make one of its findings public. Such interference in the concerns of the vast majority of humankind is frequently performed by carefully feeding certain bits of study to "outside" experts whose work and attitude have been considered to be especially worthy.

Members of the secret society, on the other hand, may feel little or no obligation to individuals outside the organization. They may just be biding their time until they can enslave the majority of humankind. For hundreds of years, some academics have been concerned about global conspiracies carried out by secret organizations waiting for the opportune time to attain full world dominance.

For twelve years, the mystery airship vanished from the sky. Then, in Peterborough, England, a police policeman reported hearing a sound akin to a motorcar above March 24, 1909. Looking above, he saw an airship emitting a bright light and moving at the speed of an express train. By July, the weird airborne contraption had been seen above New Zealand, where it lingered for six weeks before returning to the United States. There was one recorded overflight in the New England region in August. Still, the airship vanished until the night of December 12, when Long Island residents heard a buzzing sound emanating from the starlit sky above them, similar to the rattle and hum of a high-speed engine.

On January 20, 1910, the final recorded sighting of an airship occurred from Memphis, Tennessee. Several witnesses reported seeing an object flying extremely high in the air at a high rate of speed. It crossed the Mississippi River into Arkansas, then curved slightly south and vanished.

Perhaps the secret society no longer felt the need to inspire "outsiders" to pursue the science of aeronautics, because, by 1910, there had already been an international aviation competition held in Rheims, France; a flight from the deck of a seagoing cruiser; a floatplane takeoff from water; and the first woman pilot had obtained her license.

YOCKEY FRANCIS PARKER

A bizarre guy straight out of the Twilight Zone dedicated his life to reversing the outcome of World War II and declaring the Third Reich the victor.

If Francis Parker Yockey had not committed himself when the FBI eventually apprehended him in 1960, he would be thrilled with how violent and chaotic global events have gone after 9/11. He would have rejoiced in the World Trade Center's fall and in the fact that Islamic radicals were the culprits of the terrorist deed. Instead, Yockey had committed his life to alter the results of World War II, a goal he believed could be accomplished by 2050. He gave covert support to organized Muslim resistance to the West, hoping that terrorists who could not surrender would begin assaulting American cities. He envisioned a scenario in which America's worldwide hegemony would be supplanted by a European superstate modeled on Hitler's Third Reich's ideas and dominated by elitists.

Esoteric Hermetic sciences had supplanted Christianity.

Little is known about this enigmatic figure who lived on the dark fringe's darkest reaches. Just as fans of strange stories like the mystery of H. P. Lovecraft's Necronomicon, followers of fascism and Satanism like Yockey's underground work Imperium. Of course, fans of Lovecraft's work recognize that the world he built with the Ancient Ones was a work of fiction; fans of Yockey's work commit to realizing his vision of European unification under Nazi rule. Yockey dismisses the Nazi loss in World War II as a transitory setback on the path to the ultimate objective of America's isolation from European affairs and a fascist revolution in America. Imperium was created under the pseudonym "Ulick Varange" ("Ulick," allegedly a Danish Irish name; "Garage," a reference to the Norsemen) and self-published in 1948 by Yockey in a restricted edition of 200 copies. Reprints of the text are still in circulation among neo-Nazi and far-right organizations, who hold Yockey's ideas and theories in the same respect as previous like-minded readers held Hitler's, Mein Kampf.

It wasn't until a few years after Yockey's death that radical-right publisher Willis Carto released a paperback version of Imperium, and the book started to gain traction among neo-Nazi and neo-fascist organizations. Yockey's work had been commended by the Italian Hermetic philosopher Julius Evola, and Imperium was in sync with the Swiss-based New European Order and its beliefs in the mythologies of Aryan origins in the hyperborean north and Atlantis.

Yockey was born in Chicago in 1917 to a professional-class family of German, Irish, and French Canadian descent. He was raised Roman Catholic, but when he became engaged with radical-right groups in the 1930s, he became drawn to theosophical Nietzscheanism. Yockey was drawn to the German American Bund. Still, he was also drawn to the Stalinists, Trotskyites, and Father Coughlin's semi-fascist followers—any anti-capitalist organization and comprehended the world danger posed by Jews, it seemed.

Some academics believe Yockey was a member of a German-American spy network and helped Nazi saboteurs infiltrate the United States. During WWII, he was commissioned in the United States Army. He then temporarily fled but returned to service after proving to the army that he had had a mental breakdown. He received a medical release with no suspicion of assisting Nazi spies and saboteurs during his time away from the base.

Yockey had a successful academic career at various colleges before the war, a law degree from Notre Dame, and practice. As an undergraduate, he studied at Georgetown University's School of Foreign Service. With these credentials, he could get a position with the German war crimes tribunal after the war. He was, unfortunately, hired because his pr Yockey later returned to Germany after landing a position with the American Red Cross. He quickly fled his station and was deported to the United States. Yockey had utilized his posts to obtain the US government to fund his visits to Germany to engage with the expanding pan-European fascist network.

According to conspiracy theorists, Yockey spent the 1950s amassing a dizzying assortment of identities as he went literally across the globe, doing anything he could to promote the fascist cause. He was most certainly a member of Odessa, a worldwide network of postwar Nazis and fascists. Some believe Yockey spent a significant length of time behind the iron curtain before returning to the United States for a short period to serve as a copywriter for Senator Joseph McCarthy. In addition, Yockey is known to have spent time in New Orleans preparing propaganda for use in Latin America, and many conspiracy theorists believe he knew Lee Harvey Oswald at the time.

Yockey was approached by the FBI in Oakland, California, in 1960, after his various identities and passports triggered several red flags. Yockey attempted to flee before federal officials could interview him, hurting one agent in the process. Yockey died on June 17, 1960, from self-administered potassium cyanide.

OSAMA BIN LADEN

The CIA's "Frankenstein monster" studied his terrorist lessons so well that he became the most sought guy on the planet.

Osama bin Laden was the world's most sought man. The US Department of State's Rewards for Justice Program gave a prize of up to $10,000.

The Airline Pilots Association and the Air Transport Association were prepared to provide an extra $2 million to exchange information, leading to apprehension. In 1988, bin Laden founded the terrorist organization al-Qaeda ("the Base"), which funded the terrorist bombings of the United States embassies in Nairobi, Kenya, and Dar es Salaam, Tanzania, which killed 224 people (August 7, 1998); the attack on the USS Cole in Yemen (October 12, 2000); and the coordinated plane hijackings and assaults on the World Trade Center and the Pentagon (September 11, 2001). In 1998, bin Laden established the World Islamic Front for Holy War against Jews and Crusaders and issued a proclamation declaring the killing of Americans, civilians, and military alike as an "individual duty for every Muslim" to "liberate the al-Aqsa Mosque and the Holy Mosque and for their armies to move out of all the lands of Islam, defeated, and unable to threaten any Muslin."

Osama bin Laden was born in Saudi Arabia in 1957, the son of a rich Saudi family. When his father died, he inherited $300 million, and he earned a large personal fortune as a well-connected businessman in the building trades and retail commerce in the Middle East. He stood six feet four or higher and wore the clerical vestments of a spiritual leader over his exceedingly slender frame.

Conspiracy theorists find immense irony in Osama bin Laden's deadly career. He was, in their opinion, the "Frankenstein monster" produced by the Central Intelligence Agency. The CIA recruited bin Laden in 1979 to resist the Soviet invasion of Afghanistan as part of the greatest covert operation in CIA history. The CIA used Pakistan's Inter-Services Intelligence (ISI) as go-betweens since none of the CIA's efforts could be traced back to Washington for this covert activity to succeed. While there was considerable sympathy for the Afghan independence fighters, the main purpose was to devastate the Soviet Union's armed capabilities.

Bin Laden started funneling money to the mujahideen battling the invaders and grew connected to the Egyptian Jihad and other Islamic extremist organizations. The CIA aggressively pushed Afghan rebel Muslims to proclaim jihad against the Soviets, and 35,000 Muslim fanatics from forty Islamic nations were recruited to fight the invaders of their brothers' motherland. The CIA and ISI established guerrilla training camps in which military methods were combined with Islamic teachings. Bin Laden was actively engaged in training camps for freedom fighters to combat the Soviets in the early 1980s. He recruited thousands of Saudi Arabia, Algeria, Egypt, Yemen, Pakistan, and Sudan to continue the battle against Islam's enemies.

The CIA and ISI were rewarded for their covert efforts by persuading over 100,000 overseas Islamic extremists to join the resistance against the Soviet invasion. In addition, President Ronald Reagan approved a National Security Decision Directive in March 1985, increasing covert military help to the Muslim rebels.

The reactions of Muslim radicals may gauge the undercover operation's effectiveness after the Soviets withdrew; many subsequently said they had no clue they were waging war on behalf of the US. Despite interactions at the highest levels of the intelligence system, the Islamic rebels in the field had no idea that Americans were supplying them.

With advanced weapons and training to make them more effective fighters, Even the quick bin Laden stated that he saw no proof of American support in the struggle against the Soviets.

Although the Soviet Union withdrew its soldiers in 1989, the civil conflict in Afghanistan continued unabated. The Taliban (the word translates simply and humorously as "students") were finally able to impose a hard-line Islamic government in Afghanistan with the help of different forces inside Pakistan. The Taliban Islamic State benefited America's geopolitical goals at the time. Because the Afghan opium trade was funding and arming the Bosnian Muslim Army and the Kosovo Liberation Army, Washington turned a deaf ear to the screams for help from the Taliban's reign of terror.

Bin Laden created al-Qaeda in 1988 to unite Arabs fighting against the Soviet invasion of Afghanistan. It wasn't long, though, before he came to think that al-Qaeda should be the voice of the world's nearly one billion Muslims who think their concerns have gone unheard by the West.

After a truck bombing near Dhahran, Saudi Arabia, in 1996 killed nineteen US airmen and injured 515 people, including 240 Americans, bin Laden reaffirmed his call for jihad against Americans: "We have focused our declaration of jihad on the US soldiers inside Arabia," he said in an interview with CNN, but he warned that other attacks were imminent because of the bombing.

- According to bin Laden and several Islamic extremist organizations, the Arabs have several grievances with the West, particularly the United States:

- The impact of Western decadence poses a challenge to Arab fundamentalist cultures in the Middle East and other largely Islamic regions of the globe.

- Americans have controlled Arab politics for almost seventy years, ignoring calls for compensation for Zionist crimes in Israel and the "stealing" of Arab territory in Palestine.

- Because of the arrogance of some of the people who conquered that country, Arabs were made to feel unwanted in their previous country.

- Historically, the West exploited Arab oil until the Arabs created their oil cartel.

- Prejudice towards Arabs worldwide because of their religion and cultural views.

- Arab extremists aim to compel the whole globe to adopt Islam and form a universal Islamic theocracy.

Bin Laden was deprived of his citizenship and banished from Saudi Arabia in 1994 due to his resistance to the Saudi monarchy. He relocated his activities to Khartoum, Sudan, where he had several successful enterprises, but he was also removed from that country due to US pressure. He moved into mountain encampments in

Afghanistan in 1996 and built several training sites. He urged Americans at the time, in an interview with CNN's Peter Arnett, that if they wanted to halt the explosions within their nation, they should quit inciting the passions of millions of Muslims. Bin Laden warned that the "hundreds of thousands who have been slain or displaced in Iraq, Palestine, and Lebanon" had "brothers and relatives" who would turn Ramzi Yousef (convicted for the 1993 World Trade Center attack) into a "symbol and a teacher."

According to some scholars of bin Laden's rise to become the world's most known terrorist, August 19, 1998, U.S. missile attack in Sudan on a target that turned out to be an innocent aspirin, powdered milk, and baby food plant may have infuriated him enough to put his threats into action. 167 Muslims worshipping in a neighboring mosque were murdered in the bombing, including at least one of bin Laden's relatives. Bin Laden then extended his terror network and issued a fatwa (a religious opinion or judgment given by a competent scholar or religious authority) calling for jihad against the United States. He quickly gathered 100,000 additional volunteers.

Bin Laden was named to the American Federal Bureau of Investigation's Ten Most Wanted Fugitives and Ten Most Wanted Terrorist lists for his role in the 1998 U.S. embassy bombings. Following the World Trade Center attack in 2001, the FBI set a $25 million reward on bin Laden's head. In addition, conspiracy theorists cited the fact that twenty-four American members of the bin Laden family, along with over one hundred other highly placed Saudis, were flown out of the United States without being questioned as evidence that the secret government was keeping an eye on the bin Laden family.

On September 23, 2001, in response to military operations on al-Qaeda in Pakistan, Osama bin Laden said, "We pray that these brothers are among the first victims in Islam's war in this period against the new Christian-Jewish crusade headed by the grand crusader Bush under the banner of the Cross."

Osama bin Laden was able to avoid the U.S. military under three presidential administrations. However, on May 2, 2011, the fleeing al-Qaeda commander was shot and killed inside a private residential complex in Abbottabad, Pakistan, by US Navy SEALS and CIA agents in a covert attack authorized by President Barack Obama. Bin Laden's corpse was prepared for burial according to Muslim religious standards within hours, and he was buried at sea. On May 6, 2011, Al-Qaeda accepted the death of their leader and spiritual mentor and promised to strike against Americans wherever they may be located across the globe.

Bin Laden had not been given final rites, and his remains had just been buried at sea for a few days when conspiracy theorists started to circulate their claims. They suspected that the killing of the master terrorist had not gone as planned, as indicated in the official US report.

Some said that Osama was still alive and had fled the attack on his house. Others echoed a common idea that had circulated long before the SEALs murdered the terrorist leader, claiming that bin Laden died of health concerns many years before. Top al-Qaeda officials have kept tales of bin Laden sightings alive as a propaganda tactic. Even supposed CIA operatives disseminated the idea that bin Laden died in July 2001 of Marfan syndrome in Dubai.

The fact that no images of bin Laden's corpse were made available to the media for dissemination to the general public was a major flaw in the official reporting of his murder. The fact that bin Laden was buried at sea raised more suspicions about his death. Skeptics all across the globe asked to see bin Laden's corpse as the final confirmation that he was indeed dead.

Conspiracy theorists also made much of the significant disparities in the stories of the confrontation with the SEALS at bin Laden's residence. According to initial accounts, the SEALS engaged in a forty-minute shootout with bin Laden's bodyguards before seizing the compound and killing the main terrorist as he sought to use his wife as a human shield. But, according to later reports, when the SEALS invaded a rubbish-strewn complex rather than a multi-million dollar home, just one guy defended bin, Laden.

Skeptics also questioned the interviews done with residents of the bin Laden compound in Abbottabad after the operation. The vast majority of respondents claimed they had never seen bin Laden in the years he was alleged to have been there, and they were unaware of any proof that he had ever lived among them. It was particularly surprising that bin Laden could have remained unnoticed in the area for so long, given that Abbottabad functions as a staging site for the Pakistani military, akin to West Point in Pakistan. Moreover, people contended that the White House could have chosen almost anybody to act as a dummy bin Laden for the SEALS to kill and bury at sea.

For many years, conspiracy theorists claimed that Osama bin Laden was tremendously beneficial to sections of the hidden government. According to conspiracy theorists, after the globe has had enough battling terrorists, the public will resort to the New World Order for deliverance from turmoil. Meanwhile, defense contractors are becoming more wealthy, and the military is becoming more dominant.

CATHARS

The Cathars were a hidden group of Satanists who intended to demolish France's medieval church.

The Cathars, also known as the Albigensians, were based primarily at Albi, a town in the French region of Languedoc, where an official Roman Catholic Church council denounced the sect as heretics in 1208. The majority of the Albigensian settlements were looted, then destroyed, along with their documents and libraries and evidence of precisely what the Cathars thought was extracted via terrible torture. Modern study shows that, far from being the wicked creatures that Pope Innocent III (c. 1161–1216) declared should be murdered, the Cathars were devoted, chaste, tolerant Christian humanists who despised the medieval church's worldly excesses. Similar beliefs may be found in Gnostic gospels, Essenic teachings unearthed at Qumran, and Egyptian mystery schools. The Cathars referred to themselves as the True Church of God, although they did not have a set, defined theological doctrine. The majority of the rare manuscripts that escaped the Inquisition's fires were written in Provençal, the ancient language of southern France.

The remainder is in Latin, except France.

The cultural life of the Albigenses vastly outstripped that of any other town in Europe at the time. Objective historians are superior in terms of manners, morality, and education.

The Albigenses deserved more respect than the orthodox bishops and clergy, according to the state. The court of Toulouse was widely acknowledged to be the hub of a greater degree of civilization than existed elsewhere in Europe at the time.

The Cathars, according to Pope Innocent III and many members of the church hierarchy, were teaching the fundamentals of witchcraft. Even though they concentrated their faith on Christ, they saw him as a pure spirit who had fallen from heaven on the orders of the God of Good to free people from the realm of matter. The Cathars believed that since Christ was pure spirit, he did not die on the cross, and therefore, the church's doctrines were erroneous. The Cathars denied the Catholic sacraments and held that the God of the Old Testament was the king of matter and the ruler of this world, titles designated for Satan by the Catholic Church. Not only was God adored by the church as the Creator revealed to be the devil, but the Cathars also taught their followers that the majority of the patriarchs and prophets described in the Old Testament were demons. They also thought that Satan created the material world following his banishment from heaven when God the Father, pitying his once-brilliant star Lucifer, granted him seven days to see what he could conjure up. Adam and Eve's bodies were animated by fallen angels and instructed by Satan to have offspring who would follow the serpent's ways.

To combat the devil's craving for flesh, the Cathars advocated chastity, vegetarianism, and nonviolence. They believed in a gradual theory of reincarnation, in which animal souls evolved into humans. They saw the world as a dualistic realm in which good and evil had equal strength, and they saw their time on Earth as a fight to oppose Satan's might.

Innocent III proclaimed the Cathars heretics in 1208 and sentenced to death the residents of the Albigensian cities of Béziers, Perpignan, Narbonne, Toulouse, and Carcassonne as "enemy of the Church." Simon de Montfort (c. 1160–1218), a seasoned military commander, was tasked with leading a crusade against fellow Christians, sophisticated men, and women of southern France, whom the pope saw as a bigger menace to Christianity than the Islamic warriors who battled the Crusaders. Even though it took him over twenty years of fighting against the besieged Albigenses, de Montfort was able to murder 100,000 men, women, and children before being slain during the second siege of Toulouse.

Montségur, the final stronghold of Albigensian resistance, collapsed in 1244, and hundreds of Cathars were burnt at stake. The Inquisition had established its headquarters in the once highly educated city of Toulouse, and the few Cathars who had escaped execution throughout the brutal decades of the crusade launched against them were now at the mercy of the witch and heretic hunters.

GOVERNMENT OF THE ZIONIST OCCUPATION

Anti-Semitic organizations think that Zionist Jews dominate the US government.

Zionist Occupation (also Occupied, Occupational) Government (ZOG) is a phrase used by anti-Semitic organizations that claim Zionists dominate the US government. When used by a white supremacist organization, the word is usually a disparaging term for "Jew," implying that the government is controlled by Jews who are part of a worldwide conspiracy like the one revealed in The Protocols of the Learned Elders of Zion. More precisely, the phrase refers to any Jew or non-Jew who prioritizes Israel's aims above those of the United States and attempts to encourage the US government to employ military or diplomatic means to achieve those objectives.

Economic power on Israel's behalf Far-right organizations who oppose ZOG often praise the "liberation movements" of Syria, Libya, Iran, and Palestine. Yasser Arafat was seen as an especially outstanding character.

According to certain anti-semitism scholars, the term "Zionist Occupation Government" was most likely coined by Aryan Nations, which has used the ZOG reference widely in its writings and promoted it online. Others believe the word was first used in a 1976 track titled "Welcome to ZOG-World" by neo-Nazi Eric Thomson. In addition, a December 27, 1984, story in the New York Times reported on a string of robberies conducted in California and

Washington State by white supremacists who used their loot to fund a fight against the United States government, which they dubbed the "Zionist Occupation Government."

The "Aryan Declaration of Independence," which was released on the Aryan Nations website in 1996, declared that the ZOG's objective is "the installation of an absolute tyranny" over the United States, with "the annihilation of the White race and its culture" as "one of its principal purposes." Since then, the phrase has been adopted by a variety of anti-Semitic and white nationalist organizations.

FOUNDATION CHALCEDON

Rousas John Rushdoony, the originator of Christian reconstructionism, urged conservative Christians to seize control of American and global governments.

Rousas John Rushdoony (1916–2001) was a brilliant academic. He read and annotated a book every day, six days a week, for twenty-five years. Unfortunately, such a greedy reading regimen did not occupy every waking hour of his life. Rushdoony received a master's degree in English from the University of California, Berkeley, before entering the Presbyterian ministry and performing a mission to the Chinese in San Francisco and the Western Shoshone tribe in Idaho. He also published works on politics, education, law, philosophy, and conservative Christianity. Rushdoony relocated to the Los Angeles region in 1965 and established the Chalcedon Foundation, named after the Council of Chalcedon in 451, which declared that the governmental framework of the Roman Empire should be abolished.

The state must be God's servant.

Rushdoony's magnum work, The Institutes of Biblical Law, was released in 1973, an eight-hundred-page wake-up call to Protestants to begin applying biblical legal ideas to the actual world around them. Rushdoony was dubbed the "Father of Christian Reconstructionism" after issuing a major appeal to fundamental Christians to seize control of American and global governments. In 1981, he was a member of the Coalition for Revival, a group devoted to "reclaiming" America and Beverly and Tim LaHaye, Rev.

Donald Wildmon, and Dr. D. James Kennedy.

The Chalcedon Foundation's Beliefs

- For the free market and voluntary social activity to thrive, the Ten Commandments must be the organizing basis of civil governance. Christians must seize control of the government of the United States and implement strict biblical rules.

- Practicing homosexuals should face the death sentence.

- There should be no such thing as interracial marriages or forced integration.

- The Bible acknowledges that some individuals are born to be slaves. Despite current attempts to make whites feel guilty, slavery in the pre–Civil War United States was kind.

- The Holocaust did not occur in that Jews who "give false testimony" depict the claimed extermination camps.

THE LAMB OF GOD'S CHURCH

Murderous Mormon groups have waged a brutal, covert religious war, inflicting havoc. vengeance on persons who have been considered to be sinful in God's sight

According to Mormon historian Tom Green, over twenty deaths of polygamous sects have been motivated by religious views.

By a desire to acquire competing prophets' financial fortunes, congregations, and many brides And the murders seen by police and the general public may be merely a subset of the total number of fatalities. Since 1981, at least a dozen more cult members have vanished without a trace.

The killings network revolves around the now-deceased Ervil LeBaron, and expelled polygamist who claimed himself to be God's prophet on Earth and took the moniker "One Mighty and Strong." LeBaron set out a plan for execution for "traitors"—members of competing factions in Utah, Arizona, Texas, California, and Mexico—in a book of "New Covenants" that he composed while in jail.

Ervil was so vicious that he had his pregnant daughter slaughtered for opposing him, and he had his brother Joel assassinated to smooth the way for his ambition to become God on Earth. Daniel Ben Jordan, the man suspected of Joel's killing, was assassinated in October 1987. He had made the terrible mistake of leaving the protection of nine of his wives and twenty-one of his children out deer hunting. Jordan's corpse was discovered in the state's south, according to Utah police lieutenant Paul Forbes. Jordan had been shot twice in the head and twice in the chest with a 9-mm pistol. When he exited his hunting camp, he found someone waiting for him.

Jordan's assassination, a self-styled prophet apostle of the Church of the Lamb of God, was merely one in a series of unexplained slayings that remain shrouded in mystery.

Mormons practiced polygamy until the late 1800s. Then, when Utah was attempting to become a state, the church decided to end the practice of having numerous wives. Several organizations, however, split from the original Church of Jesus Christ of Latter-day Saints and created their interpretations of Mormonism. Each sect was headed by a person who claimed to hold the keys to power. As a result, many of the groups fled to Mexico, Arizona, or California.

One such group of fundamentalists established "Colonia Juárez" in Chihuahua, Mexico. Ervil LeBaron grew up in this colony.

Polygamists, a farmer's son dismissed from the orthodox Church in 1924 due to his odd views and teachings. In 1944, Ervil and his six brothers were excommunicated.

Following his father's death, Joel LeBaron said that he had the Key of Power and established the Church of the Firstborn of the Fullness of Time. Joel announced himself to be God's prophet and asked that all of his demands be fulfilled and followed without inquiry.

Ervil wasn't convinced that Joel was true, and since Ervil had the privileged position of producing the majority of the sect's literature, he could record the facts as he saw them. He determined that Adam was God and that the Holy Ghost was Joseph Smith, the founder of Mormonism. Ervil also said that the theology of blood atonement required the execution of all offenders. Furthermore, he imagined the One Mighty and Strong ruling over all Mormons.

Detective Forbes said that Ervil distributed letters declaring that he was the ultimate authority and that all group members were required to pay tithes to him. Joel had had enough of such disobedience by 1970. Ervil was deemed unstable by him, and he was removed from his position as sect head. Undaunted, Ervil established the Church of the Lamb of God and declared himself to be the true One Mighty and Strong. In little time, he had thirteen wives and was on his way to a bloody campaign.

Police have proved that from this point on in the covert battle, heinous acts proceeded at a breakneck pace:

Joel LeBaron is assassinated in Mexico on the orders of his brother in August 1972.

In December 1974, a commando-style raiding group of men and women firebombed the Mormon settlement of Los Molinos in Mexico. As a result, two people are murdered, while fifteen others are injured. The raid is claimed to have been commanded by Ervil LeBaron.

Ervil concludes that Naomi Zarate, the wife of one of his disciples, was disobedient in January 1975. Soon later, she vanishes and is never seen again.

Robert Simons of Grantsville, Utah, contests Ervil's claim and proclaims himself the One Mighty and Strong in April 1975.

However, Simons departs, and it is assumed that he was executed.

One of Ervil's military leaders, Dean Vest, feels horrified by the executions and murders and plans to defect in June 1975. But, instead, he is assassinated in his sleep.

Ervil is arrested in Mexico in March 1976 for his role in Joel's killing. After eight months, his twelve-year sentence is dramatically overturned, and he is freed. However, while in jail, he gains new admirers, including heroin dealer Leo Peter Evonik.

Ervil informs his followers in April 1977 that his daughter Rebecca has revolted against him. He has her strangled and buried in a mountain hole.

Dr. Rulon Allred, head of Utah's biggest polygamist sect and Ervil's main challenger for the title of God's Prophet, is assassinated in Murray, Utah, in May 1977. LeBaron sends a kill crew to Allred's burial, but the shooters flee when they see strong police protection. They run to Texas to avoid Ervil's anger for the mission's failure.

May 1979: Ervil is apprehended by Mexican authorities, extradited to Utah, and prosecuted and convicted for the murder of Allred and a machinegun assault on his brother Verlan LeBaron.

Ervil LeBaron is discovered dead in his cell at Utah State Prison in August 1981.

According to the official report, he died of a heart attack.

Verlan LeBaron was murdered in a suspicious vehicle collision in Mexico in August 1981.

Brenda Lafferty and her infant daughter, Erica, are discovered dead in their house in American Fork, Utah, the victims of a ritual slaying. Their necks were so badly cut that their heads were almost decapitated.

Leo Peter Evoniuk, 52, presiding patriarch of the Millennial Church of Jesus Christ, goes missing while on a business visit in Watsonville, California, in May 1987.

Daniel Ben Jordan, fifty-three, prophet apostle of the Church of the Lamb of God, is attacked while deer hunting in southern Utah in October 1987.

Lieutenant Forbes stressed that the persons executing the brutal covert battle should be viewed as clan chieftains, rather than most polygamous Mormons, normally law-abiding and low-key people who do not want to create any type of noise.

According to law enforcement, around thirty thousand persons are in 10 organizations like Ervil LeBaron's across the southern states and Mexico. These organizations engage in power contests to take over one another's financial bases. If they assassinate competing prophets, many of the deceased's followers are likely to flock to them. Some of the organizations are exceedingly affluent. Some, like Ervil's bones, are poor. They are, however, all incredibly private and tight.

AGENCY OF CENTRAL INTELLIGENCE

Name practically any conspiracy, and the CIA is almost certainly involved in some manner.

Only die-hard Bush loyalists were astonished when the CIA published a series of secret files updating their prewar intelligence assessments on Iraq's weapons of mass devastation (WMD). Any American with a pulse recalls the president warning the country shortly after the horrors of September 11, 2001, that "intelligence reports" stated Iraq has significant stocks of chemical and biological weapons and was striving to achieve nuclear capability. CIA intelligence findings served as the primary reason for the 2003 invasion of Iraq, validating the necessity for the US to launch a preemptive attack. According to the book Plan of Attack by journalist Bob Woodward,

CIA Director George Tenet informed President Bush that discovering WMDs in Iraq would be a "slam dunk."

"The CIA has now conceded that their estimations of WMD were incorrect," Representative Jane Harman of California, the House's top Democrat,

Reuters obtained a statement from the Intelligence Committee. She also urged CIA officers to engage in aggressive information gathering on Iran and North Korea, "both of which are known to have active WMD programs."

The Central Intelligence Agency (CIA) was established in 1947 to replace the Office of Strategic Services (OSS), which had served the United States throughout World War II. The Agency's mission was to acquire information, steal the Soviet Union's secrets, and foil Soviet operatives' operations. But, then, it was the Cold War, with the iron curtain, brainwashing tactics, subtle Communist propaganda, and a threat from a Soviet leader to bury us.

The CIA's purpose and mission statements are intended to instill trust in the Agency's honesty and righteousness: "Our Vision—To be the cornerstone of a world-class intelligence community in the United States, renowned for both the high quality of our work and the excellence of our people. Our Mission—As ordered by the presidents, we conduct counterintelligence, special operations, and other foreign intelligence and national security tasks. Accepting responsibility for our actions is how we do our work. We strive for continuous development in all we do."

Conspiracy theorists aren't buying the CIA's flag-waving, lofty boasts about its "vision and purpose." According to whistleblowers inside the government and abroad, the US government has routed hundreds of billions of dollars via the Agency since the early 1950s to pay the nation's wars, covert operations, and covert military programs. This is the shadow government's dark underbelly. The only option for these covert projects to receive the funds they need without causing a national budget shortage that would elicit public outrage is to engage in illegal activities. Our government battled in Southeast Asia, beat the Taliban in Afghanistan, and invaded Panama to depose Manuel Noriega to maintain its major interests in the drug trade in these places. The CIA takes hundreds of billions of dollars every year for covert projects. The CIA is active in drug operations in Southeast Asia's Golden Triangle and Golden Crescent and south of the US border, such as Panama and Colombia. The renegade CIA operates barely underneath the radar. It is reportedly implementing these initiatives to safeguard America's wealth and power.

Conspiracy theorists know that the US government has managed and controlled numerous foreign nations for decades via the CIA. It has often killed or disenfranchised foreign leaders of sovereign countries and created puppet administrations that serve our interests.

For fifty years, the CIA has also performed covert chemical and biological tests on the American people, injecting individuals, spraying portions of cities, and infecting civilians. Without their knowledge, up to 500,000 individuals have been used as guinea pigs by the government. Soldiers, minorities, drug users, jail populations, homosexuals, even whole populations of large U.S. cities have been indiscriminately utilized. Since 1998, conspiracy theorists have accused the hidden government of spraying "chemtrails" over the sky of the United States, allowing mysterious substances to fall on the populace.

The murder of President John F. Kennedy, who was intending to end the Vietnam War and declaw the CIA, is perhaps the most often mentioned black project of the CIA and rogue forces inside the Pentagon, together with members of the Mafia and anti-Castro Cubans. However, conspiracy theorists think that rogue individuals inside the CIA performed, planned, helped organize, or had prior knowledge of several other evil initiatives and nefarious activities. The following are some of the most repeatedly labeled bad businesses by conspiracy theorists:

- Martin Luther King Jr.'s assassination; Robert F. Kennedy's assassination

- the murder of most of the Black Panther leadership; George Wallace's attempted assassination

- Control of opium shipments in Laos and Vietnam; substantial domestic monitoring of US persons

- causing thousands of people to be killed in Vietnam and Indonesia; sparking revolutions and conflicts in minor states across the world; Iran-Contra;

- Iraq's covert armament in its battle against Iran; Hundreds of billions of dollars have been stolen from savings and loan institutions.

- tens of thousands of deaths done by death squads operating as vigilantes

- Proxies from the United States

Michael Parenti writes in Dirty Truths: Reflections on Politics, Media, Ideology, Conspiracy, Ethnic Life, and Class Power that the CIA is by definition conspiratorial. The CIA may use "covert acts and hidden schemes, many of which are of the most heinous kind." What, after all, are covert operations if not conspiracies?"

According to conspiracy theorists, the ultimate objective of the most elite and secretive secret organizations has always been to concentrate all economic and political power into a new worldwide network entirely controlled by the New World Order. To achieve this aim, they must dethrone the United States from its current economic and political strength. Thus, their current goal is to destroy us from within.

CHURCH OF SATAN

On April 30, 1966, Anton Szandor LaVey established the First Church of Satan in San Francisco, ushering in the Age of Satan.

Anton Szandor LaVey (1930–1997) shaved his head, assumed black clerical attire, replete with white collar, and declared himself Satan's high priest on April 30, 1966 (Walpurgisnacht, a night legendarily cherished by the devotees of evil). LaVey openly declared that the Age of Satan has begun. It was the dawn of magic and pure insight, and he benefited from it.

In San Francisco, he founded the First Church of Satan.

Belief in magical abilities or worship of Satan were not novel concepts. What was novel was LaVey's use of the word "church" in the title of his organization. There were marriages, burials, and children christened in the name of Satan, in addition to rites and rituals dedicated to the Prince of Darkness.

When LaVey, the head priest of the Satanic Church of America, married socialite Judith Case and freelance writer John Raymond, he conducted the ceremonies over a nude lady who functioned as the live altar. Later, when LaVey described the meaning of the rite,

He told reporters that an altar should not be a cold, hard slab of sterile stone or wood. Instead, it should represent unfettered passion and excess.

The first public marriage ceremony in the United States by a demonic sect was quite a spectacle. The bride eschewed the conventional white gown in favor of a vibrant red gown. The groom donned a black turtleneck sweater with a matching coat. However, the high priest stole the show with a black cloak lined with scarlet silk and a blood-red hood with two white horns protruding.

In 1969, LaVey released The Satanic Bible, which affirmed the beliefs of the Church of Satan and declared Satanism to be "dedicated to the evil, hidden power in nature responsible for the workings of earthly events for which science and religion have no explanation." He said that he was inspired to start the Religion of Satan because he saw a need for a church that would "recapture man's body and carnal impulses as objects of celebration." The First Church of Satan does not acknowledge Satan as a real entity but rather a metaphor of materialism. The church maintains that Satan represents an inner attitude and should never be seen as an object onto which human abilities are projected to worship what is merely human in an externalized form.

The Satanic Bible is organized into four divisions or volumes, representing one of the four occult elements: fire, air, earth, and water. The first part, titled "Book of Satan," instructs the reader that "ponderous rule books of hypocrisy are no longer required" and that it is time to rediscover the Law of the Jungle. The "Book of Lucifer," the second portion, discusses how the Roman deity Lucifer, the light bearer, the spirit of enlightenment, became linked with evil via Christian beliefs. The "Book of Belial" is a fundamental treatise on ritual and ceremonial magic written in Satanist terminology. Finally, the "Book of Leviathan," the fourth part, emphasizes the significance of the spoken word ineffective magic.

Satanist philosophy glorifies man as an animal. It elevates sexual hunger above spiritual love, believing that the latter is a charade. According to Satanism, aggression must be responded to with violence, and loving one's neighbor is a utopian unreality. Satanists see prayer and confession as useless, futile gestures, thinking that the only way to attain one's goals is via sorcery and relentless effort—and that the greatest way to relieve oneself of guilt is to avoid it in the first place. If Satanists make a mistake, they acknowledge truly that err is human. Instead of attempting to wash, they investigate the circumstance to find precisely what went wrong and how to avoid it from occurring again. They think that studying and performing rituals highlighting humankind's sensual nature and channeling this power toward the discharge of psychic or emotional energy is the path to higher degrees of personal perfection and an examination of life's deeper secrets.

Because Christian religions, particularly the Roman Catholic Church, are considered anathema to the Prince of Darkness, Satanists utilize parodies of Christian rites and symbols in their rituals. The cross, for example, is employed, but the long beam is facing downward. Likewise, Satanists may employ the pentagram or five-pointed star, which is generally associated with Wicca or witchcraft; however, like the cross, it is inverted, resting on a single point rather than two. Satanists believe that their parodying and inversion of other faiths' rituals and symbols are not done just for the goal of blasphemy; rather, such usage appropriates and inverts the power inherent in the ritual or symbol for Satan's aims.

The Satanic Bible outlines nine criteria for defining Satanism in the modern day. Satan stands for:

1. indulgence rather than abstinence;

2. vital life, rather than ethereal pipe fantasies;

3. pure knowledge, rather than dishonest self-deception;

4. compassion to those who deserve it, rather than love spent on jerks;

5. revenge, rather than turning the other cheek;

6. accountability to the accountable, rather than worry about psychological vampires;

7. Man as merely another animal, more often than not worse than animals that walk on all fours, who, as a result of divine spiritual and intellectual growth, has

    1. become the most ferocious beast on the planet;

8. any so-called transgressions that result in bodily, mental, or emotional enjoyment;

9. the Church's greatest friend ever since he has kept it going all these years.

LaVey quickly gained media attention, often letting reporters see rites he performed over the live altar of a woman's nude body at his church, the famed "Black House," which was formerly a brothel. Attention from movie stars, employment as a technical consultant on films like Rosemary's Baby, and the hatred of millions of ardent

Christians, who viewed LaVey as a form of antichrist, all came at once. After a few years of death threats and persecution, LaVey went underground, canceled all public events, and rebranded his religion as a secret organization.

In 1991, a court-ordered LaVey sold the "Black Horse," along with memorabilia such as a shrunken head and a stuffed wolf, and share the money with his estranged wife, Diane Hagerty.

On October 30, 1997, LaVey died the day before Halloween. His estate immediately became the subject of a court battle between his eldest daughter, Karla, and Blanche Barton, his lifelong partner and the mother of his son Xerxes. (LaVey's younger daughter, Zeena, left the Church of Satan and became a priest in the Temple of Set in 1990.) The First Church of Satan is still active today, led by High Priestess Blanche Barton and Magister (High Priest) Peter H. Gilmore.

When questioned recently about New Testament experts' finding that the long-feared number of the Beast of Revelation may be 616, rather than 666, Magister Gilmore stated that Satanists would always utilize anything that frightens Christians. It makes no difference if the number is 616 or 666; the Satanist will employ whichever is most despised.

TSUNAMI IN ASIA IN 2004

Conspiracy theorists quickly identified anything from a covert military operation to aliens correcting the Earth's spin as possible causes of the devastating tsunami.

A 9.3 magnitude earthquake shook the ocean bottom off northern Sumatra early on December 26, 2004, causing billions of tons of saltwater to rise. Giant waves surged toward Sumatra, Thailand, and Sri Lanka beaches, crashing down on thousands of unsuspecting locals, holiday revelers, and international visitors. The huge tsunami killed possibly 300,000 people and proceeded on its deadly path until it expended all of its force on the Kenyan beaches

Only a few days after the horrible event, conspiracy theorists all around the globe were busy discrediting experts' claims for a natural disaster. These people contended that this was not an act of God but rather an intentional act of cruel men. The following were some of the most popular theories:

The US military had been quietly developing a lethal eco weapon.

Electromagnetic waves wreaked havoc on the ecosystem and provoked the earthquake that resulted in the tsunami.

One of the superpowers had tested an undersea nuclear bomb that proved to be much more powerful than expected.

The United States military and State Department had obtained early notice of the oncoming tsunami, but they did little to warn Asian nations.

All of the world's governments were aware of the impending monster tsunami but did nothing to warn the victims in its path to comply with the New World Order's goal to reduce planetary population.

Beneficial aliens had observed that the earth's rotation had become uneven and unsteady and attempted to fix its orbit. Finally, after the tsunami, scientists in India determined that the planet's rotation had grown more stable.

THE AMERICAN PROTECTIVE ASSOCIATION

In response to a purported Roman Catholic plot to seize control of the United States, the APA established a secret club to keep all Catholics out of public office.

The American Protective Association (APA) was an underground proscriptive club in the United States that worked to keep Roman Catholics out of political office. During the 1890s, the organization became an unpleasant presence on the political landscape in most northern states, but it had limited effect in the south.

Except for a few members in Georgia and Texas, the South.

On March 13, 1887, Henry F. Bowers, a sixty-year-old lawyer from Maryland, formed the APA in Clinton, Iowa. Bowers, a Mason, drew liberally from Masonic rituals to create elaborate regalia, initiation rites, and a secret oath binding members to strive at all times "to place the political position of this government in the hands of Protestants, to the complete exclusion of the Roman Catholic Church, of its members, and the mandate of the Pope." The APA capitalized on Protestant prejudice about Catholics to garner membership. Many Masons, who already barred Catholics from their fraternal organization, joined the drive to keep Catholics out of public office.

In 1893, the APA started actively disseminating anti-Catholic material and organized public talks by acting as ex-priests who revealed the Catholic Church's heinous secrets. Some of these forgers claimed to have witnessed a papal bull calling for the slaughter of Protestants on or around the Feast of Saint Ignatius in 1893. By 1894, the APA had seventy weekly tabloids.

Slanderous lies about the Catholic Church The assertion that Terence V. Powderly, the commander of the Knights of Columbus, was heading that Catholic group in a huge plot against all American institutions was prominent among the reports.

Bowers was re-elected as the APA's national president in 1898. Still, the organization had failed to influence any significant changes in government laws or policies. It gradually faded, leaving only a legacy of animosity between Catholics and Protestants vulnerable to allegations of Catholic plots.

COINTELPRO: THE FBI'S COVERT WAR AGAINST AMERICA

In our youth, we thought the FBI stood for truth, justice, and the American way. However, Director J. Edgar Hoover granted his agents free rein to pursue some extremist groupings.

To oppose the expanding radical movements of the 1950s, 1960s, and 1970s, the FBI and police expanded their legally permitted powers in what they saw as legitimate abuses of constitutionally given individual liberties. J. Edgar Hoover, director of the FBI, directed his field agents to "expose, disrupt, misdirect, discredit, and otherwise neutralize" certain target organizations. The American Indian Movement, the Communist Party, the Socialist Workers Party, black nationalist groups, Students for a Democratic Society, and a wide range of antiwar, antiracist, environmentalist, feminist, Lesbian and gay groups were among the groups deemed disruptive to the fabric of American society. Martin Luther King Jr. and any group that sought social or racial justice, such as the NAACP, came under specific assault.

Many organizations, including the Lawyers Guild and the American Friends Service Committee, are involved.

In the extreme, covert operations were used. The field agents' mission was not just to spy on group leaders and report any "un-American acts" but also to disparage them personally and ruin their reputations.

Those who have always thought of the FBI as upholding the greatest standards and staunchly protecting truth, justice, and the American way would be very disappointed to find that FBI agent working on Hoover's instructions engaged in such heinous and criminal crimes as the following:

- false and defamatory reports regarding radical leaders were often planted in the media;

- Forged signatures on personal communication and public documents; produced and distributed fictitious flyers in the names of their target groups;

- made anonymous and provocative phone calls to prominent persons pretending to be leaders of targeted organizations demanding social or racial justice;

- Meetings of numerous organizations were announced, with inaccurate dates and hours published;

- Posing as members of radical or civil rights organizations, set up false cells to gather information on the kind of people drawn to such organizations.

- False arrests were performed to get criminal records for the leaders and members of the targeted organization;

- Perjured testimony and manufactured evidence were used in court, resulting in unjust convictions.

- To intimidate certain targeted organizations, particularly black, Puerto Rican, and Native American activists, FBI agents, and police officers threatened physical violence, broke into and destroyed organization offices, and delivered savage beatings.

The Citizens Committee to Investigate the FBI succeeded in removing classified papers from an FBI office in Media, Pennsylvania, and releasing them to the public in early 1971. The domestic counterintelligence program (COINTELPRO) of the FBI was revealed. That same year, the Pentagon Papers, top-secret government documentation on the Vietnam War, were made public. Several FBI agents started to quit from the agency, revealing more heinous truths about COINTELPRO. High-ranking government officials were made uneasy by revelations that the FBI had used "dirty tricks" on American citizens just because they held antiwar rallies or marched and sat-ins for social and racial justice. The coordinated assault on people's rights, reputations, and lives was condemned as acts of government terrorism.

Senate and House committees launched thorough investigations into the tactics used by the government to acquire information and conduct covert operations. These hearings exposed extensive unlawful operations involving the FBI, CIA, and other government agencies.

United States Army Intelligence, the White House, the Attorney General, and state and municipal law enforcement were used against people who challenged domestic and international policy.

Even though the COINTELPRO scandal resulted in a temporary reform of government abuses in the 1970s, official secrecy has been reinstated. The Freedom of Information Act, which was crucial in revealing operations like COINTELPRO, was repealed by the Reagan administration via administrative, judicial, and legislative acts. According to civil rights advocates, many of the covert criminal acts carried out during COINTELPRO were approved by Executive Order 12333 on December 4, 1981. Worryingly, what was authorized is most likely still being practiced.

WILLIAM COOPER

Milton William Cooper: an authority in UFOs?
Are you a conspiracy theorist? Are you a member of the Navy
Intelligence Service? Is there a controversial radio personality?
Militia commander? Survivalist? Patriot? Fanatic?
Who is America's most dangerous man?

William "Bill" Cooper (1943–2001) was a famous conspiracy theorist and patriot. He spoke out regarding the Constitution, the JFK murder, the Trilateral Commission, the Bilderberg Group, the Illuminati, the New World Order, UFOs, and the One World Government.

Cooper's extensive investigation into the information he "stumbled on," along with his top-secret military credentials, propelled what he came to feel was his mission. For more than ten years, he talked and taught in every state in the country and across the globe, all while devising as many methods and means as possible to keep his findings in the public view. His desire to distribute information or "disseminate the truth," as he viewed it, became his life purpose.

Cooper rose to international prominence as a radio personality with The Hour of the Time (or HOTT), a WBCQ global shortwave radio show he established and hosted for one hour every Monday through Thursday night. He often said that speaking out the enormous risks he was taking would be mitigated by going public with as large an audience as possible. That way, he said, if he were "taken out permanently," people would have to think that he was an intentional target to be silenced. The more people who heard his radio broadcasts, saw his video productions, listened to his cassettes and lectures, or read any or all of his many publications, including newspapers, newsletters, and books, the better—even if it meant his death. "Wake up, folks, don't trust me or anybody else; investigate it for yourself," he was always challenging his audience to conduct their research and form their own opinions.

Cooper cautioned that any registration, whether it includes goods, social security, or gun regulation, is a tool devised to collect information on individuals to enslave them ultimately. He spoke ceaselessly about the overarching goals of the covert One World Government. Furthermore, it is claimed that credit cards, driver's licenses, bank accounts, and other such items are all part of the

He angrily encouraged listeners to be informed that almost all data—even medical data—would be encoded into an obligatory computer chip or similar monitoring device and implanted in each person entirely reliant on and subject to the hidden government. All monetary transactions, including income, purchases, and even taxes, will be coded via these chips. No one will be able to make a livelihood or buy or sell anything without one implanted.

Cooper maintained that if our society and each individual in it acted honestly and with purity, such a Big Brother system would not be threatening; however, due to the malicious intentions, desires, and greed of some elitists, the ultimate manipulation and total rule over the masses would be disastrous.

Cooper's lectures were supplemented by papers, graphics, and extensive research, and he frequently hammered home one of his most vexing points: it is illegal to force individuals to pay taxes. Moreover, he contended that it is illegal to proclaim it necessary for residents to pay taxes, citing the Declaration of Independence and the Constitution as evidence that the United States of America has been a republic from its creation. This was one of his primary reasons, and it was also one of the most deadly. "We Americans have mindlessly and faithfully succumbed to this, and it is wrong," he would scream.

Cooper was raised in an air force family and moved from town to town and nation to country. Thus he was schooled in, lived in, or traveled in most of the world's major nations, giving him a global perspective. In his adult years, he had a distinguished military career, holding several top-secret clearances that would later prove to be instructive in ways he had not anticipated. He joined the United States Air Force's Strategic Air Command, where he had a secret clearance and worked on B-52 bombers, refueling planes, and Minuteman missiles for a while until receiving an honorable discharge. His desire to join the navy had previously been dashed due to motion sickness. Having overcome that illness, he enlisted in the navy after leaving the air force, participating in submarine duty during some of the most difficult years of the Vietnam War. In Vietnam, he also took part in port patrol and river security operations, and he was decorated for his bravery and leadership during battle.

Cooper also served on the intelligence briefing team for the Pacific Fleet's commander in chief and as a petty officer of the watch at the Command Center in Makalapa, Hawaii, where he maintained a Top Secret, Q, SI security clearance. After receiving an honorable discharge from the navy in 1975, he continued his study. He earned an associate of science degree in photography and worked as the executive director of Adelphi Business College, among other things. He was also the marketing coordinator for National Education and

Software. These ventures equipped him with the experience and abilities he eventually employed in creating and promoting his films when his true calling became clear to him.

Cooper's audacious comments and claims drew the attention of government officials. Knowing this, he always maintained that he would rather go out in a blaze of glory than remain silent. Seeing a huge clash on the horizon, Cooper took his family out of the country in March 1999 for their safety. He stayed in his Eagar, Arizona, home to finish his job, accompanied only by his "guard geese," two dogs, one rooster, and one chicken. Cooper was shot and murdered during a raid on his residence by the Apache County Sheriff's Department on November 5, 2001.

There are usually conflicting accounts of any given situation, and this one is no exception. Several sheriff's office accounts indicated that the incident was not a planned SWAT raid on Cooper's house but rather a simple "confrontation" between the police and Cooper that culminated in an exchange of gunfire. Robert Martinez, an Apache County officer, was also badly injured. According to some stories, the gunshots occurred during an attempted arrest. In any event, many of Cooper's listeners and supporters think the event was simply the murder of one of the first individuals to expose the government for what it is. Although admitting that Cooper was not an easy man to get along with, these supporters believe that the authorities withheld evidence about the shootout, and claims along these lines have since served as provocative fodder for those screaming that his "murder" was itself a conspiracy—to silence Milton William Cooper once and for all.

MOVEMENT FOR CREATIVITY

The Creativity Movement is a religion that believes exclusively in the white race and does not believe in God, heaven, hell, or everlasting life.

Even though the Creativity Movement's slogan is "RaHoWa" (Racial Holy War),

War) declares itself a racial religion. As members of the organization are known, creatures do not believe in God, heaven, hell, or everlasting life. According to the Creators, if you are of the white race, you already have everything. You are, after all, "nature's ultimate creation." "What is beneficial for the white race is the greatest virtue; what is harmful to the white race is the ultimate sin," according to the Creators' interpretation of the Golden Rule.

Ben Klassen launched the Creativity Movement in 1973 as the Church of the Creator (COTC). Born in Ukraine and raised in Canada, Klassen was a member of many far-right groups, including the John Birch Society, which he eventually condemned. He was the Florida chairman of George Wallace's 1968 presidential campaign. He worked on a book called Nature's Eternal Religion, which he hoped would replace the Judeo-democratic-Marxist values that were poisoning contemporary life with a new concept of race as a transcendent embodiment of absolute truth. Christianity, on the other hand, was a suicidal faith. At seventy-five, Klassen committed himself on August 6, 1993, by eating four bottles of sleeping tablets.

Klassen's life was not going well as he neared the end. He had a few followers to his new religion, but on May 17, 1991, one of the COTC clergy, George Loeb, killed a black Gulf War veteran and was sentenced to life in prison with no chance of release for the next twenty-five years. The dead sailor's family, backed by the Southern Poverty Law Center, filed a $1 million vicarious culpability claim against the COTC in 1992. Klassen urgently tried to sell all of his assets and disassociate himself from the COTC. His initial candidate for taking over as group head served a six-year term for supplying contaminated meat to public school cafeterias. The second choice was a pizza delivery guy from Baltimore, but at the last minute, the job was filled by a Milwaukee skinhead who managed COTC until January 1993. Klassen replaced the skinhead with Richard McCarty, telemarketing, just before his death in August 1993.

Under McCarty's direction, the COTC floundered. Less than a year after Klassen's death, the Southern Poverty Law Center filed a lawsuit to dissolve the

The Creator's Church, McCarty turned over swiftly.

Matt Hale became aware of COTC while attending Bradley University in Peoria, Illinois, in the early 1990s. Still, he showed no significant interest in joining the organization until he saw a chance to take leadership in 1995. Hale had been attracted to Hitler and National Socialism since he was a child, and he had studied Mein Kampf and the literature of racist groups since he was in the eighth grade. On July 27, 1996, Hale's twenty-fifth birthday, a panel of COTC elders known as the Guardians of the Faith Committee appointed him pontifex Maximus, or "highest priest," of the organization, which he renamed World Church of the Creator (WCOTC). Hale infused the organization with fresh vitality and attracted many young male followers to the WCOTC, many of whom became committed members.

Hale graduated from Southern Illinois University with a law degree and passed the bar test in 1999. However, due to his well-recognized racism, the state bar revoked him a license to practice. As a result, Hale utilized this denial as yet another marketing gimmick. He appeared on various radio talk shows and tabloid television shows hosted by Ricki Lake, Leeza Gibbons, and Jerry Springer. In addition, on an NBC broadcast titled "Web of Hate," Tom Brokaw featured him.

In 1999, Benjamin Smith, a member of the WCOTC, embarked on a two-state killing rampage that began on July 4, murdering two people and injuring nine others, all of whom were members of ethnic and religious minorities African Americans, Asian Americans, and Jews. Hale first denied knowing Smith, but after meditating on the devastation caused by Smith, he said that the whole loss was just one white guy.

The WCOTC lost a copyright infringement action launched against them in November 2002 by the Te-Ta-Ma Truth Foundation, trademarked "Church of the Creator" many years earlier. Hale failed to comply with U.S. District Court Judge Joan Humphrey Lefkow's order to stop using the name Church of the Creator on websites and other printed material. When he arrived in court for a contempt of court hearing in January 2003, he was arrested for plotting to assassinate the judge.

Judge Lefkow went home from work on March 7, 2005, to discover her husband, attorney Michael F. Lefkow, and her mother, Donna Humphrey, dead in pools of blood, apparently killed with gunshot wounds to the head. Matt Hale was immediately accused of arranging and directing the killings.

As an act of retaliation against the judge, he escaped from his detention cell. Hale maintained his innocence, and he was declared not guilty in this case after Bart Ross, who was upset with Judge Lefkow for rejecting a malpractice action he had filed, wrote a suicide note admitting to the killings. In planning to kill Judge Lefkow in 2003, Hale got a forty-year jail term on April 6, 2005.

Ben Klassen created The White Man's Bible in 1981, which became obligatory reading for all Creativity Movement members. Among the principles contained in Klassen's "Bible" are the following:

- Nonwhites, or "mud races," are subhuman and the White Race's natural adversaries.

- Jews are the white race's deadliest adversary, attempting to "mongrelize" it to realize their ultimate historical aim of completely enslaving all races on the planet.

- Christianity is a Jewish "concoction" meant to intimidate the childishly naïve with the notion of damnation and to terrify them into servitude.

- All meaningful culture and civilization are the work of white people.

- Whether religious, political, or racial, every problem must be evaluated through the White Man's eyes and "exclusively from the point of view of the White Race as a whole."

ATLANTIS

Atlantis was a magnificent lost society with superior technology than our own, as well as a Golden Age that inspired dozens of secret organizations and thousands of dreamers, poets, mystics, and daring archaeologists.

Ignatius Donnelly (1832–1901) wrote Atlantis: The Antediluvian World in 1882, suggesting that every civilization is a descendant of Atlantis. Donnelly argued that the traits they shared resulted from contact with Atlanteans, members of the ancient civilization who escaped destruction during its catastrophic final days and managed to impart their knowledge to other world peoples, helping civilize primitive societies and passing on the secret cult of Atlantis. Among the constructions are the pyramids of Egypt and the Americas, the Sphinx of Egypt, and the megaliths of Western Europe.

ascribed to the Atlanteans' brilliance

Believers have attributed the Atlanteans with possessing the capability to manufacture electricity, create flying machines, and harness nuclear power for energy and warfare in the years after Donnelly's controversial book was released.

More than 9,000 years before such items, they existed in contemporary culture. Some allege that the Atlanteans knew about a powerful death ray, levitation secrets, and pure forms of energy via crystals. Many Atlantis believers think that the residents of the lost continent had cosmic links with extraterrestrials and that the lost continent was a colony founded on Earth by alien explorers.

Undersea divers exploring the area near Bimini Island in the Bahamas in the late 1960s discovered what appeared to be roadways, walls, and buildings under the water in the exact location prophesied by Edgar Cayce (1877–1945), a widely admired psychic whose "life readings" for clients revealed that many of their present-life psychological traumas resulted from terrible incidents that the individuals witnessed. According to Cayce, much of their difficulties stemmed from their experiences as inhabitants of Atlantis.

Cayce contributed to popularizing a modernized vision of Atlantis as a sophisticated culture capable of inventing aircraft, submarines, X-rays, antigravity technologies, crystals that harness solar energy, and strong explosives. He hypothesized that a dreadful explosion in 50,000 B.C.E. separated Atlantis into five islands, followed by another rupture in 28,000 B.C.E. and a third in 10,000 B.C.E. Cayce said that he was an Atlantean priest circa 10,500 B.C.E. who foresaw the approaching devastation and sent some of his disciples to Egypt to guide the construction of the Sphinx and the Pyramids.

Cayce prophesied in 1940 that fragments of Atlantis would resurface in the Bahamas in the late 1960s. Two pilots spotted a rectangular object in the water off the coast of Andros, the Bahamas' biggest island, in 1967. Next, divers discovered another stone structure in the form of a "J" off the coast of Bimini. The J-shaped feature was thought to represent a stone path. Extensive diving trips were regular in the region, and some divers claimed to have spotted temple, pillar, and pyramid fragments.

Atlantean enthusiasts believe that the governmental, ecclesiastical, and scientific authorities conspire to conceal Atlantis evidence from the general public. They claim that if the existence of the ancient sophisticated civilization were formally accepted, present assumptions about the history and evolution of humanity would have to be radically changed. Acceptance of a primordial super civilization would jeopardize the existing civilization.

Understanding of history has become outmoded. Finding indisputable proof of a great global culture that flourished while the rest of humanity struggled to exist on a rudimentary level would undermine traditional understanding of civilization's growth.

Plato (427–347 BCE) characterized Atlantis as a state of perfect order and a model civilization in his writings. He describes the island continent and how Atlanteans conquered all known globes save Athens in two of his dialogues, Timaeus and Critias. Critias, named for Plato's great-grandfather, the principal speaker in the conversation, offers a history of Atlantean civilization and depicts the perfect society that existed there. According to Critias, the tales were handed down through his ancestor, Solon (615–535 B.C.E.), a statesman and poet who traveled extensively.

Egyptian priests in the Nile Delta city of Sais taught Solon that there was once a place even older in history than Egypt, which the Greeks accepted as being centuries older than their own culture. The priests detailed Atlantis, a great island continent that flourished some eight thousand years before and was situated beyond the Pillars of Hercules, the Greek designation for the cliffs that form the Strait of Gibraltar, the Mediterranean Sea's westernmost point. The Atlantic Ocean lies beyond the strait. The main metropolis, also known as Atlantis, was situated amid a series of concentric rings that alternated between strips of land and sea. The water rings acted as trade routes and contributed to forming a set of natural barriers that made

Atlantis exceedingly difficult.

Although Atlantis possessed a large force of professional troops, the culture encouraged them to study, which resulted in improvements in engineering and science that made the continent abundant, attractive, and powerful. A network of bridges and tunnels connected the land circles, and intelligent exploitation of natural resources brought security and plenty. Many trees gave peace and beauty, racetracks were utilized for sporting tournaments, and irrigation systems maintained abundant crops.

According to Plato, the inhabitants of Atlantis ultimately grew corrupt and greedy, prioritizing personal interests above the greater good. To gain global dominance, they started invading neighboring countries. Poseidon, the sea god, was enraged by these developments and destroyed the civilization, hammering the continent with earthquakes and floods until the ocean swallowed up Atlantis.

Some have related the widespread narrative of Atlantis' demise to other apocalyptic occurrences, such as legends of a vast deluge in the Bible, the Epic of Gilgamesh, and flood myths in other nations. In addition, some argue that the end of the Ice Age between 12,000 and 10,000 B.C.E. led to global water level increases and earthquakes, volcanic eruptions, and temperature changes that were either accidental or related to the Ice Age.

the epoch associated with the demise of Atlantis

In December 2001, explorers using a miniature submarine to probe the seafloor off the coast of Cuba announced the discovery of stone structures deep beneath the ocean surface that were suggestive of ruins left by unknown civilizations thousands of years ago, compelling fans of the lost continent. According to representatives of the Canadian-based Advanced Digital Communications and scientists from the Cuban Academy of Sciences, the buildings were spread as if they were relics of an urban area at a depth of roughly 2,100 feet. The ancient metropolis beneath the water was estimated to be over 6,000 years old, around 1,500 years before Egypt's renowned Giza pyramids. Whether this interesting find is Atlantis or evidence of a land bridge that formerly connected Cuba to mainland South America, it will be contentious.

ANTICHRIST

For many Christians, the greatest of all conspiracies will be those perpetrated by the antichrist against the disciples of the resurrected Christ.

Although the term "antichrist" is generally connected with Revelation's apocalyptic New Testament book, it appears nowhere in that text. The epistle writer claims in 1 John 2:18 that the "enemy of Christ" has appeared and that many false professors have entered the Christian ranks. In verse 22, John identifies anybody who denies Jesus as the Christ, the Father, and the Son as the antichrist, and in 2 John 7, he claims that there are many deceivers currently in action among the believers

In Matthew 24:3-44, Jesus goes into considerable detail with his followers regarding false messiahs and prophets who would fool many people with stories about the end of the world. He refers to the prophet Daniel and his warnings about the end times, and he warns the disciples not to follow false prophets.

Teachers who will perform amazing miracles and signs to deceive God's chosen ones. No one, not even the angels, knows when the Son of Man will return on the clouds of heaven, Jesus says.

The oldest incarnation of the antichrist is presumably the warrior king Gog, who appears in Ezekiel and returns in Revelation with his kingdom of Magog, signifying Satan's earthly henchmen who would assault God's people in a last great fight of good vs. evil. According to Jewish literature regarding the "end of days," the armies of Gog and Magog will be destroyed, and the world will finally be at peace.

Throughout the Bible, the antichrist is the Son of Perdition, the Man of Sin, the Man of Lawlessness, the Prince of Destruction, and the Beast. The guy is described in great detail by the prophet Daniel: he would be a wicked ruler who will "exalt and elevate himself above every god and will talk outrageous things against the God of gods." But at his estate, he would (secretly) venerate a deity of forces and a divinity unknown to his forebears. Thus he shall do in his citadel with a new god, whom he shall recognize and magnify; and he shall reign over many and divide the country for gain" (Dan. 11:36–39).

The wicked king, the antichrist, is connected with ten kings who pledge their authority and loyalty to him to build a short-lived empire of violence and ruin in both Daniel and John the Revelator's prophecies: "And the ten horns of this kingdom are ten kings who shall arise: and another shall arise after them, and he shall be diverse and speak great words against the highest God, and shall wear down the saints of the Highest One, and shall think to change times and laws: and they shall be given into his hand for three and one-half years" (Dan. 7:24).

Although Jesus explicitly states that no one knows the hour or day of His Second Coming, Christian scholars have consistently viewed the rise of the antichrist to earthly power as a kind of catalyst that will set in motion Armageddon, the final battle between good and evil, the ultimate clash between Jesus Christ's armies and Satan's armies. So Christians have been around for millennia.

Endeavored to find the antichrist among their day's great and brutal leaders, such as Nero, Napoleon, Hitler, Mussolini, and Stalin Nominations for the job have often been influenced by political or religious prejudices: the pope has been a favorite of evangelicals for the humiliating title since the Protestant Reformation.

The number 666 is associated with the antichrist according to Revelation 13:18, which declares that the number of the Beast is 666 and that this number represents a person. In John, the Revelator's first-century reality, the Beast that dominated the globe would have been Nero, the Roman Empire's emperor, and caesar. Using the Hebrew alphabet, the numerical value of "Caesar Nero," the ruthless persecutor of the early Christians, is 666.

Scholars disclosed on May 1, 2005, that a newly found piece of the earliest surviving copy of the New Testament, dating from the third century, suggests that subsequent copyists got it wrong: the Beast's number is 616. According to David Parker, professor of New Testament textual studies and paleography at the University of Birmingham in England, Figure 616 relates to another foe of the early Christians, the emperor Caligula.

Those who believe the number 666 is still a powerful predictor of the antichrist will continue to suggest modern contenders for the position. For example, the numerical value of Franklin Delano Roosevelt's name was reputedly 666. Since he served as President of the United States for twelve years—during the Great Depression and World War II—many of his conservative Christian adversaries started to see him as the antichrist. Even Ronald Wilson Reagan, considered by many political experts to be one of our country's most popular presidents, had some critics point out that he had six letters in each of his three names—666.

The epithet "antichrist" has been used by so many people in popular culture in recent decades that it has lost much of its meaning and feeling of threat. However, fundamentalist Christians who believe strongly in the coming Tribulation, Apocalypse, Rapture, and the grand final battle of good versus evil at Armageddon believe that the title of antichrist retains its fear factor and that we must pay close attention to the Beast's signs and warnings as prophesied in the book of Revelation.

MUTILATIONS OF CATTLE

Extraterrestrials mutilate cattle and remove their tongues and genital parts to get enzymes that will allow them to exist on Earth.

According to several forensic pathologists who have examined maimed cattle with their tongues, eyes, ears, anuses, udders, and genitalia removed without spilling a drop of blood, traditional surgical tools had not been used.

The cuts looked to be the product of cutting-edge laser technology.

Several veterinarians and forensic professionals who have analyzed the strange mutilations have characterized the blood as looking to be contaminated.

It was drained with no vascular breakdown as a consequence. But, unfortunately, the technology that could handle such a feat does not exist on Earth, and even if it did, it would need extensive, heavy equipment to manage creatures that may weigh more than 1,500 pounds.

Traces or marks of a traditional type, such as tire imprints or human or animal tracks, have never been discovered near a corpse, according to most tales of cow mutilation; nonetheless, numerous farmers and ranchers have claimed the indentations of a tripod nearby. In addition, several claims of UFOs or unmarked black helicopters have been claimed in the area previous to the tragedy.

This sort of animal mutilation seems to be widespread, with the same animals being targeted as victims. According to reports from Argentina in July 2002, over two hundred cattle had been discovered with their blood drained and tongues, organs, flesh, and skin removed by angular, precisely curved incisions, commencing with the first reported mutilation in April. Argentine farmers often identified UFO teams as the most probable mutilators of their livestock herds.

Many skeptical veterinarians, livestock association officials, forensic pathologists, chemists, and a slew of the county, state, and federal officers and agents believe that such alleged mutilations are simply Mother Nature carrying out one of her primary responsibilities, that of keeping the countryside clean. According to these investigators, the genuine offenders of the mutilations are predators and scavengers.

UFO experts dismiss the likelihood that predators or scavengers could incise and take certain organs from their victims in such a precise manner. However, the apparent difficulty with blaming predators and scavengers is that the remainder of the animal is still alive.

Linda Moulton Howe, the author of Glimpses of Other Realities, is the most well-known animal mutilation researcher (1998). Howe has recorded hundreds of unusual, unexplainable deaths of animals on the open range, especially cattle and horses, all of which had bloodless excisions of eyes, organs, and genitals.

Howe feared pollution in the environment when she started her intense investigation in the autumn of 1979, and that some government agency was surreptitiously taking tissue and fluids for evaluation. But

She couldn't understand why any government organization operating in secret would be so irresponsible as to leave cow corpses lying in fields or ranges, causing fear and outrage among the animals' owners. Howe's first interviews were with ranchers and law enforcement authorities, who grudgingly told her about sightings of luminous disks around the mutilations. Some witnesses even reported seeing otherworldly beings at the location. However, her ongoing investigation has persuaded her that something peculiar is going on, which might entail extraterrestrial experiments on Earth's creatures.

According to certain UFO/conspiracy theorists, around 1954, a shadow organization inside the United States government struck a deal with extraterrestrial intelligence that allowed animal mutilation and human abductions in return for superior alien technology. The aliens explained the cow mutilations by saying that their evolutionary climb had rendered their digestive systems defective. As a result, extraterrestrials would be best able to survive on Earth by consuming an enzyme, or hormonal secretion, most easily acquired from cow tongues and throats.

HISTORICAL MYSTERIES

The Truth Behind the World's Most Perplexing Events and Conspiracies Revealed – Mind-Blowing Stories of Four History's Mysteries and Conspiracy Theories!

BERNADINE CHRISTNER

THE ESCOVEDO MURDER

'M any a man may trace his downfall to a murder, of which, perhaps, he thought little enough at the time,' writes De Quincey. This comment refers especially to Philip II. of Spain, his secretary, Antonio Perez, Perez's steward, his page, and several professional ruffians. From the King to his scullion, everyone was involved in the assassination of Juan de Escovedo, the secretary of Philip's famed natural brother, Don John of Austria. All of them, to varying degrees, had deep reasons to regret an action that seemed to be a routine political occurrence at the time.

The mystery in the case of Escovedo is neither the method in which he disappeared nor the identities of his killers. These facts are widely known; the identities of those responsible, from the King to the bravo, are known. However, obscurity obscures the motivations for the action. Why was Escovedo executed? Did the King slay him for merely political motives, which were insufficient in the first place but were inflated by the suspicious royal fancy? Or were Philip II's secretary and Spain's monarch competitors for the love of a high-ranking one-eyed widow? And did the secretary, Perez, persuade Philip to order Escovedo's killing because Escovedo threatened to divulge their wicked plot to the King? With varying degrees of agreement, Sir William Stirling-Maxwell and Monsieur Mignet accepted this interpretation. Mr. Froude, on the other hand, believed Philip acted for political motives and with the full consent of his ill-informed conscience.

According to Mr. Froude, there was no woman as a motivation in the case. A third possibility is that Philip wanted to kill Escovedo for political reasons, without regard for the sensitive affection. Still, Philip was hesitant and indecisive, while Perez, who feared Escovedo's involvement with his love affair, spurred his royal master on to the crime he was avoiding. We may never know the whole truth, but we may study a condition of morality and manners in Madrid that makes the blundering tragedies of Holyrood in Queen Mary's time seem like child's play. When put against Philip II's instruments, Bothwell's 'lambs' are lively and compassionate.

Escovedo, the slain man, and Antonio Perez, Shakespeare's "first killer," had both been schooled in the service of Ruy Gomez, Philip's famed minister. Gomez had a wife, Aa de Mendoza, who, having been born in 1546, was thirty-two, not thirty-eight (as M. Mignet claims) when Escovedo was assassinated in 1578. However, 1546 might be a typo for 1540. She was blind in one eye in 1578, but both of her eyes were undoubtedly bright in 1567 when she seems to have been Philip's mistress or was widely assumed to be. Eleven years later, at the time of the murder, there is no reason to believe Philip was still susceptible to her charms. Her husband, Prince d'Eboli, had died in 1573 (or, as Mr. Froude says, in 1567); the Princess was now a widow, and if she chose to distinguish her husband's old secretary, at this date the King's secretary, Antonio Perez, there seems no reason to suppose that Philip would have been bothered by the matter. M. Mignet's view of the sufficient cause of Escovedo's murder is that he still loved Aa with an unroyal fidelity, that she loved Perez, and that she and Perez feared Escovedo would betray them to the King. Mignet, on the other hand, believes, and correctly so, that Philip had made up his mind, as far as he ever did, to assassinate Escovedo long before that diplomatist became an uncomfortable spy on the alleged lovers.

To get things up to the tragic level of Euripides' Phdra, Perez was believed to be the natural son of his late boss, Gomez, the spouse of his supposed lover. Perez was most likely nothing of the such; he was the bastard of a man of his name. His supposed mistress, Gomez's widow, may have even disseminated the other tale to establish that her ties with Perez, albeit personal, were innocent. They are a lovely group of folks!

Escovedo and Perez have been buddies since they were children. While Perez moved from Gomez's service to Philip's, Escovedo was appointed secretary to the nobly daring Don John of Austria in 1572. The Court thought he was supposed to be a spy on Don John, but he succumbed to the charms of that brave heart and gladly accepted, if not inspired, the most audacious designs of the winner of Lepanto, the Sword of Christendom. This was highly uncomfortable for the leaden-footed Philip, who never took time by the forelock, but instead brooded on projects and passed up opportunities. Don John, on the other hand, was all for pressing the game. When he was dispatched to tempt and conciliate in the Low Countries and remove the Spanish army of occupation, he planned to transfer the Spanish men out of the Netherlands via water. He would descend on England once they were on the blue sea, rescue the prisoner Mary Stuart, marry her (he was fearless!), reestablish the Catholic faith, and assume the English crown. A solid plan, authorized by the Pope, but one that did not fit Philip's mind. He set his leaden foot on the concept and several other brave undertakings designed in the finest Alexandre Dumas tradition. Now, to whom Don John was devotedly attached, Escovedo was the essence of all these chivalrous schemes, and Philip saw him as a very dangerous person as a result.

When Don John first visited the Low Countries, Escovedo was in Madrid (1576). He persisted in pressing Philip to adopt Don John's ardent suggestions, despite Antonio Perez's requests to be careful. Perez was Escovedo's buddy on this day, 1576. But Escovedo was not to be counseled; instead, he sent an agitated letter to the King, criticizing his stitchless policy (descosido), dilatory, shambling, and idealess operations. According to Sir William Stirling-Don Maxwell's John of Austria, "the term employed by Escovedo was descosido, unstitched." However, Mr. Froude claims that Philip subsequently repeated the phrase regarding another letter from Escovedo, which he also referred to as a "bloody letter" (January 1578). Mr. Froude is unlikely to be correct here since Philip's letter containing that filthy term was written in July 1577.

In any event, Philip was persuaded to ignore the error in 1576 by Perez's pleading, and Escovedo, whose presence Don John sought, was sent to him in December 1576. Don John and Escovedo began writing to their friend Perez on this day, and Perez enticed them by showing their letters to the King. Just as Charles I. commissioned the Duke of Hamilton to spy on the Covenanted nobility, pretending to sympathize with them and speaking in their holy manner, Philip gave Perez instructions to capture Don John and Escovedo. 'I want no theology but my own to defend myself,' Perez remarked, and Philip responded, 'My theology takes the same view of the problem as yours.'

According to M. Mignet's hypothesis, at this time, 1577, Perez, although a gambler and a profligate who accepted gifts from all hands, must have intended nothing worse than serving Philip as he liked to be served to keep him fully informed of Don John's ambitions. According to M. Mignet, Escovedo was not yet an impediment to Perez's and the King's mistress, Princess Eboli's amours. On the other hand, Sir William Stirling-Maxwell believes that Perez's goal was to destroy Don John; Sir William admits that he does not know why. On the other hand, Perez had no such goal until Don John confided in him initiatives that were subversive or hazardous to the Government of his lord, the King.

Did Don John, or Escovedo, entrust Perez with plans that were not only chivalrous and impractical but also traitorous? Don John, on the other hand, did nothing of the like. Escovedo abandoned him and traveled to Spain without being summoned, arriving in July 1577. Don John beat the Dutch Protestants at the battle of Gemblours on January 31, 1578, while he was away. He then addressed a letter to Escovedo and Perez in Madrid, full of chivalrous devotion. He would make Philip the true lord of the Low Countries, and he urged Escovedo and Perez to instill resolve in the King. That was unthinkable because Philip could never have wanted to assassinate Escovedo just because he had pleaded for assistance for Don John. Yet, as soon as Escovedo announced his return to Spain in July 1577, Philip remarked in a letter to Perez, 'we must dispatch him before he kills us.' There seems to be no question that the letter in which this sentence appears is real, even though we only have a copy of it. The sentence, however, appropriately translated? 'priest á despacherle antes que nos mate' (Escovedo) translates as 'we must be swift and dispatch him before he kills us.' Mr. Froude, who is far kinder to Philip than to Mary Stuart, recommends translating the line "we must dispatch Escovedo promptly" (i.e., send him on his way) as "before he scares us to death." Mr. Froude so disputes that Philip intended to assassinate Escovedo in 1577. If the King uttered the words twice, it is bad for Mr. Froude's argument and Philip's reputation. In March 1578, he wrote to Perez about Escovedo, telling him to 'act fast before nos mate—before he murders us.' At least, that's what Perez said, but is his date correct? Perez did act this time, and Escovedo was slaughtered! If Perez is correct, Philip meant what he stated in 1577 when he declared, 'Despatch him before he murders us.'

Why did Philip fear Escovedo so much? We only have Perez's public words in his description of the incident. Perez adds a unique allegation against Escovedo after explaining the basic reasons for Philip's fear of Don John and the notions that a very skeptical monarch would have entertained, given his brother's adventurous nature. According to Perez, he pledged that after conquering England, he and Don John would invade Spain. Escovedo requested the captaincy of a castle perched on a cliff overlooking Santander's harbor; he was the town's alcalde. He and Don John intended to utilize this citadel against their ruler so that Aramis and Fouquet intended to exploit Belle Isle in Dumas' book. In truth, Escovedo had requested the leadership of Mogro, the castle controlling Santander, in the spring of 1577, and Perez notified Philip that the site should be improved for the safety of the harbor, but not given to Escovedo. Don John's allegiance could never have imagined the use of the location as a stronghold to be held in the event of an assault on his King. But, if Perez held no resentment against Escovedo in 1577 as being harmful to his purported amour with the Princess Eboli, then Philip's deadly plot must have sprung from the deep suspiciousness of his temperament, not from Perez's promptings.

Escovedo arrived in Spain in July 1577. He was not slain until March 31, 1578, despite many attempts on his life a few weeks before. M. Mignet contends that Philip held his hand until the early spring of 1578 because Perez calmed his fears; that Escovedo then threatened to reveal Perez's love affair to his royal rival; and that Perez, in his private interest, now changed his tune and, instead of appeasing Philip, urged him to commit the crime. But Philip was so sluggish that he couldn't even perform a murder with reasonable haste. Even in his view, Escovedo was not dangerous while he was apart from Don John. But as the weeks passed, Don John maintained demanding Escovedo's return by letter. For that reason, maybe, Philip pushed his bravery to the (literally)'sticking' point, and Escovedo became stuck.' On the other hand, Major Martin Hume claims that conditions had changed, and Philip had no reason to kill.

M. Mignet and Sir William Stirling-Maxwell, Don John's biographer, have quite different perspectives. They claim that in 1578, Princess Eboli was Philip's lover; she duped him with Perez, that Escovedo threatened to reveal everything, and that Perez then murdered Philip. Would Escovedo have consistently accepted Perez's dinner invites if this had been the case? If Escovedo were threatening Perez, the men would have been on the worst of terms, yet Escovedo continued to dine with Perez. Again, Perez's approach would have been to send Escovedo where he wanted to go, to Flanders, far away from Don John. It is likely, but not proven, that the Princess and Philip were lovers around 1567. However, it isn't very certain, and not proven, that Philip was still dedicated to the woman in 1578. The Mendozas, some of the Princess's relatives, now intended to assassinate Perez as a disgrace to their heritage. Later, during Perez's trial, substantial evidence proved that he loved the Princess or was suspected of doing so, but it is not established that this was an issue that Philip was concerned about. Thus, it is not impossible that Escovedo despised Perez and the Princess's relationship, but nothing suggests that he might have put himself at risk by disclosing them to the King. Furthermore, if he had spoken his thoughts to Perez about the affair, the two would not have continued on terms of the most amicable contact, as they seemed to have done. A Perez squire recalled a scenario in which Escovedo threatened to condemn the Princess, but how did the squire become a witness to the episode in which the Princess challenged Escovedo with great coarseness?

In any case, when Philip contacted the Marquis of Los Velez about the appropriateness of executing Escovedo rather than returning him to Don John, the Marquis was persuaded by ordinary political suspicions.

It was a matter of conscience at the time as to whether a king might have a subject slain if the royal motivations, though substantial, could not be exposed safely in a court of law. On these grounds, Queen Mary had the authority to detain Darnley for good political reasons that could not be made public; for international reasons. On the other hand, Mary did not consult her confessor, who felt she was innocent of her husband's murder. Philip's confessor informed him that the King had complete authority to dispatch Escovedo, and Philip delivered his instructions to Perez. According to Perez, he reiterated his comments from 1577 in 1578: 'Make haste before he murders us.'

In this matter of conscience, the authority of a king to inflict murder on a subject for political purposes, Protestant thinking seems to have been forgiving. When the Ruthvens were assassinated on August 5, 1600, at Perth, in the most enigmatic of all mysteries, the Rev. Robert Bruce, a staunch Presbyterian, refused to accept that James VI. had not plotted their death. 'But your Majesty could have hidden motives,' Bruce remarked to the King, who, of course, maintained his innocence. This seems to indicate that Mr. Bruce, like Philip's confessor, believed that a monarch had the authority to kill a subject for hidden State purposes. The concept was fiercely condemned by the Inquisition when a Spanish preacher held it, yet Knox approved King Henry's (Darnley's) murder of Riccio. On this issue, I sympathize with the Inquisition.

Perez, who had been tasked with organizing the crime, delegated the task to

Martinez serves as his steward. Martinez asked a rough-looking page, Enriquez, whether he knew "someone in my nation" (Murcia) "who would thrust a knife into a person." 'I shall talk about it to a muleteer of my acquaintance,' Enriquez replied, 'which I did, and the muleteer undertook the job.' However, when Enriquez learned that a man of significance was about to be knifed, he warned Perez that a muleteer was not noble enough and that the job must be given to individuals of greater respect.'

Enriquez confessed in 1585 for a legitimate reason: Perez had grossly mishandled the firm. All kinds of individuals were engaged, and after the murder, they fled and started to die in an alarmingly regular fashion. Naturally, Enriquez assumed Perez was behaving similarly to Mures of Auchendrane, who sent a slew of witnesses and collaborators in their assassination of Kennedy. Because they constantly required a new accomplice to murder the previous accomplice, then another to slaughter the slayer, and so on, the Mures would have depopulated Scotland if left uncontrolled. Enriquez predicted that his time to die would come soon, so he confessed, which Diego Martinez confirmed. As a result, the truth was revealed, and murderers should take note.

Perez was resolved to poison Escovedo while the muleteer hung fire. But he had no idea how to go about doing it. Science was still in its infancy for her. To poison a guy in Scotland, you had to depend on a vulgar witch or send a guy to France, at a considerable price, to get the poison, and the messenger was discovered and tortured. The Spanish Court was not more scientific.

Martinez sent Enriquez to Murcia to collect toxic plants, which a venal pharmacist distilled. The toxin was subsequently tested on a barnyard bird, which did not fare any better. On the other hand, Martinez managed to get specific water that was good to be offered as a drink.' Perez invited Escovedo to dinner, Enriquez sat at the table, and in each cup of wine Escovedo drank, he added 'a nutshell of the water,' quite homeopathically. Escovedo was no more poisoned than the previous experiment's cock. 'It was determined that the beverage had no impact at all.'

Escovedo dined with the kind Perez again a few days later. They offered him some white powder in a dish of cream on this occasion, as well as the poisoned water in his wine, considering it a shame to squander that beverage. Unfortunately, this time Escovedo was ill, and Enriquez tricked a scullion in the royal kitchen into putting more of the powder in a bowl of soup at Escovedo's dwelling. For this, the unfortunate kitchenmaid who made the soup was hung in Madrid's public Plaza, without apologies.

Is Philip was destroying the morale of his people at an alarming pace! However, it is impossible to cook an omelet without breaking eggs. Philip slaughtered the girl in his kitchen as if he had grabbed a rifle and shot her, yet the royal confessor undoubtedly declared that everything was OK.

Despite the resources of Spanish science, Escovedo continued to live, and Perez judged that he had to be shot or stabbed. So Enriquez traveled to his home country in search of an assassin and "a stiletto with a very fine blade, far better than a handgun to murder a guy with." Enriquez, to retain a good thing in the family, enrolled his brother; and Martinez, from Aragon, brought 'two suitable types of men,' Juan de Nera and Insausti, who undertook the duty with the King's scullion. Perez traveled to Alcala for Holy Week, much as the excellent Regent Murray left Edinburgh after preaching on the morning of Darnley's murder. Both gentlemen's motto was 'Have an alibi.'

On the evening of Easter Monday, the underlings pursued

Escovedo. Enriquez did not come across him, but Insausti completed his task with a single push in a skillful manner. The scullion rushed to Alcala and informed Perez, who was 'overjoyed.'

We part ways with this noble and devoted servant and move our attention to Don John. When he heard the news from afar, he had no illusions about love relationships being the root of the crime. 'In sadness greater than I can explain,' he wrote to his unhappy brother, the King. He said that the King had lost his finest servant, a "guy without the objectives and skill that are currently in fashion." 'I may have just considered myself to be the cause of his death,' the blow was aimed squarely at Don John. He showed heartfelt concern for Escovedo's wife and children, who died impoverished because (unlike Perez) 'he had clean hands.' By the love of our Lord, he begged Philip to "exercise all conceivable care to ascertain where the blow originated from and to punish it with the harshness which it merits." He will personally settle the dead's most urgent bills. (Beaumont, 20 April 1578.)

This letter most likely astounded the royal caitiff. On September 20, Don John addressed his last letter to his brother, expressing his need for a decision from your Majesty. 'Give me instruction on how to run matters!' 'I will not respond,' Philip scribbled in the margin. Don John, on the other hand, had concluded his letter. 'Our lives are on the line, and all we ask is that we die with honor.' These are the last lines of the famous Montrose's farewell letter to Charles II:

"with the greater alacrity and ardor I go to find my death." Don John, like Montrose, 'took loyalty and honor to the grave.' He died on October 1st, following a long illness. According to Brantôme, he was poisoned by the King on the orders of Perez, and the side of his breast was yellow and black as if scorched and disintegrated at the touch. When a great person died in his bed, these words were invariably said. They are most likely false, but a king who can kill his brother's friend conscientiously may also kill his brother conscientiously and for the same reasons.

Princess Eboli compensated and protected one of Escovedo's killers. They were all rewarded with gold chains, silver cups, an abundance of golden écus, and army appointments; all were transported out of the nation, and some started to die mysteriously, which, as we saw, scared Enriquez into confessing (1585).

Perez was immediately suspected. He made a sympathy call to young Escovedo: he talked about Escovedo's love affair in Flanders; an aggrieved spouse must be the guilty guy! However, skepticism grew. Perez protested to the King about being pursued, scrutinized, and cross-examined by the alcalde and his son. Vasquez, another royal secretary, was a friend of the Escovedo family. Knowing nothing of the King's guilt, and envious of Perez, he continued telling the King that Perez was guilty: that there was a courtship, discovered by Escovedo: that Escovedo died for the love of a woman: that Philip must examine the matter and put an end to the scandal. The lady in question was, of course, Princess Eboli. Philip didn't care about her anymore, at least not just now. According to Mr. Froude, Don Gaspar Moro's investigation on the Princess "has thoroughly refuted the alleged relationship between the Princess and Philip II."

On the other hand, Philip was deeply involved in property litigations against the Princess, which Vasquez handled, while Perez naturally sided with his benefactor's widow. Vasquez's letters on these topics number in the hundreds. Meanwhile, he went, and the Escovedo family fled, leaving no stone unturned in their pursuit of proof that Perez killed Escovedo because Escovedo foiled his courtship with the Princess.

Philip has often vowed to support Perez. But the affair was coming to light, and if it had to come out, Philip preferred that Vasquez pursue Perez on the wrong scent, the fragrance of the courtship, rather than the correct smell, which went directly to the throne and the wretch who sat on it. Neither approach, however, could be very appealing to the King.

Perez accepted to face trial even though no proof could be uncovered against him. His co-conspirators were far away; he would be forgiven, just as Bothwell had been cleared of Darnley's killing. Philip was unable to face the issue. He ordered Perez to consult the President of the Council, De Pazos, a Bishop, and tell him everything while De Pazos consoled little Escovedo. The Bishop, a casuist, told young Escovedo that Perez and the Princess were "as innocent as me." The Bishop disagreed with the Inquisition, claiming that

Perez was innocent because he only carried out the King's murderous orders. Young Escovedo fled, but Vasquez persisted, and in a letter to the King, Princess Eboli referred to Vasquez as a "Morish hound." Philip arrested both Perez and the Princess since Vasquez was not to be set down; his job connected with the litigations was to chase the Princess, and Philip couldn't inform Vasquez that he was on the wrong path. The lady was returned to her lands, which gratified Vasquez, and Perez and he were bound to maintain the peace. But suspicion hovered about Perez, and Philip wanted that it did. The secretary was charged with peculation, having accepted bribes on all hands, and he was condemned to huge penalties and jail (January 1585). Now that Enriquez had confessed, a type of covert investigation, the records of which still exist, dragged its plodding course. Perez was being held in residence near a church. He jumped out a window and raced inside the church, where civil force ripped open the gates, violated sanctity, and discovered our buddy cowering in the wooden work beneath the roof, all hung with festoons of cobwebs. The Church condemned the judges, but they had captured Perez, and Philip refused to submit to the religious tribunals. Perez, a prisoner, attempted to escape with the help of one of Escovedo's killers, who remained steadfast but failed, while his wife was ill-treated to force him to hand up all of the King's incriminating letters. He did, however, turn over two locked trunks full of paperwork. But his buddy and steward, Martinez, is alleged to have chosen and hidden the royal notes that proved Philip's guilt.

The King assumed he was secure now and didn't bother checking to see whether his incriminating letters were still in the sealed trunks! At the very least, if he did know they were missing and that Perez could give evidence of his guilt, it is difficult to understand why, with numerous uncertainties and hesitations, he let the covert murder procedure against Perez continue, after a lengthy pause, until 1590. Vasquez cross-examined Perez many times, but there was still just one witness against him: the scoundrel Enriquez. One was insufficient.

A new step has been made. The royal confessor informed Perez that if he disclosed the complete truth and acknowledged publicly that he had acted on royal instructions, he would be safe! When Perez disobeyed, Philip issued another instruction (Jan. 4, 1590). Perez must now divulge the King's motivation for ordering the assassination. If Philip were preparing a trap for Perez, it would only catch him if he couldn't produce the King's incriminating letters, which he still had. Mr. Froude claims that Philip learned via his confessor, and he learned through Perez's wife that the letters were still hidden and could be retrieved. If that were the case, Perez would be secure, but the King's reputation would be ruined.

What were Philip's goals and motivation? Is he going to declare the letters to be forgeries? No other person (at the time) wrote with such a different hand as his; it was the worst in the world. He must have had a loophole; else, he would not have pressured Perez to testify about his crime. He had a loophole, and Perez was aware of it, since otherwise he would have following instructions, recounted the complete tale, and been let free. He didn't do it. Mr. Froude believes he did not believe the royal power would be sufficient to satisfy the judges. But they couldn't convict Perez, a mere accomplice to Philip, without also condemning the King, which the judges couldn't do. Perez, I believe, would have preferred to take his chances with the judges' harshness against their King rather than reject the King's demand to confess everything and therefore suffer torture. He did face the torture, which suggests that he knew Philip might, in some way, avoid the terrible evidence of his letters. According to Major Martin Hume, Philip's loophole was that if Perez disclosed the King's motives for ordering the murder, they would look outmoded at the crime time. Pedro would be solely responsible. In any case, he was tortured.

Like most individuals in his situation, he underestimated his capacity to withstand pain. He lacked the stamina of the younger Auchendrane assassin, Mitchell, or the courageous Jacobite Nevile Payne, tortured almost to death by the servants of the Dutch tyrant, William of Orange. All of them endured the agony and kept their secrets hidden. But 'eight rounds of the rope' opened Perez's lips, whose obstinacy had only caused him considerable difficulty. However, he did not submit Philip's letters as evidence; instead, he claimed that they had been seized from him. However, the following day, Diego Martinez, who had previously denied everything, realized that the game was over and accepted the reality of all that Enriquez had confessed in 1585.

Perez fled about a month after the abuse. His wife was permitted to see him in jail. She had been the strongest, bravest, and most dedicated of women. If she had any cause to be envious of the Princess, which was far from clear, she had forgiven everyone. She had gone to the ends of the world to rescue her spouse. She had flung herself on the confessor of the King in the Dominican church during high mass, insisting that the priest refuse to absolve the King until he released Perez.

Admitted to her husband's jail, she performed the trick that rescued Lord Ogilvy from the Covenanters' cell, as well as Argyle, Nithsdale, and James M. Macgregor. Perez stepped out of jail wearing his wife's gown. We might assume that the guards were bribed: cooperation is always present in these situations. One of the killers had horses around the corner, and Perez, who the rack could not have seriously hurt, rode thirty miles and passed the Aragon border.

We are not required to follow his subsequent exploits. The reluctance of the Aragonese to surrender him to Castile and their rescue of him from the Inquisition lost them their constitution, and around seventy of them were burnt as heretics. But Perez was able to get away. He visited France, where Henry IV befriended him, and England, where Bacon hosted him. He published his Relaciones in 1594 (?) and informed the world of the tale of Philip's conscience. Of course, that narrative cannot be trusted, and Philip's signed letters regarding Escovedo's murder have been lost. However, the copies in the Hague are considered legitimate, and the exciting parts are marked in red ink.

If, after all, Philip had obtained the whole autograph correspondence and Perez had only succeeded in retaining the copies currently in the Hague, we can see why Perez did not confess the King's crime: he had only copies of his proofs to exhibit, and copies were worthless as evidence. On the other hand, however, Perez had the letters.

'Bloody Perez,' as Bacon's mother referred to him, died in Paris in November 1611, outliving the terrible lord he had so diligently served. Queen Elizabeth persuaded Amyas Paulet to assassinate Mary Stuart. Being a man of honor, Paulet declined; he also feared Elizabeth would leave him to the Scots' fury. Perez should have known Philip would forsake him: his stupidity was rewarded with jail, torture, and confiscation, which were hardly more than the man deserved for betraying and murdering Don John of Austria's servant.

Note.—When I wrote this article, I was unaware that Major Martin Hume had addressed the issue in Transactions of the Royal Historical Society, 1894, pp. 71-107, and in Espaoles é Ingleses, 1894, pp. 71-107. (1903). The last piece very certainly reflects Major Hume's last thoughts. He discovered several of Perez's contemporaneous letters among the Additional MSS. of the British Museum (28,269), which augment the copies of other letters burnt after Perez's death in the Hague. Based on these MSS. and other sources unknown to Mr. Froude and Monsieur Mignet (see the second edition of his Antonio Perez; Paris, 1846), major Hume's thesis This took place in late October or early November 1577. The instruction was not then carried out; the reason for the delay is unclear to me. The months passed, and Escovedo's death ceased to be politically desired under changed circumstances, but he became a major annoyance to Perez and his lover, Princess Eboli. Philip never rescinded the murder, but Perez, according to Major Hume, wrongly claims that the King was still intent on carrying it out and that another leader was contacted and approved of it soon before the actual crime. This impression is created by Perez's deft manipulation of dates in his tale. When he killed Escovedo, he was battling for his hand; but Philip, who had never countermanded the crime, remained unconcerned until 1582 when he was in Portugal with Alva. The King now knew that Perez had acted abominably, that he had poisoned his mind against his brother Don Juan, that he had disclosed State secrets to the Princess Eboli, and that he had murdered Escovedo, not in accordance to the royal decree, but as a cover for his revenge. As a result, Philip was harsh with Perez, and his last demand was for Perez to reveal the royal motivations for the destruction of Escovedo. They would be discovered to be out of date when the crime was committed, and Perez would be held accountable.

If I understand Major Hume properly, this is his hypothesis. The theory maintains Philip's moral character as dark as ever:

he ordered an assassination that he never even attempted to reverse. His confessor may cheer him, but he understood that the physicians of the Inquisition, like the general opinion of people, rejected the premise that rulers had the authority to condemn and kill, by the blade, those who had not been placed on trial in public.

MYSTERY OF THE KIRKS

No historical issue has perplexed Englishmen more than the nature of the variations between Scotland's numerous Kirks. The Southron discovered that worshipping in a church of the Established Kirk ('The Auld Kirk,') the Free Church, or the United Presbyterian Church (the U.P.'s) was the same thing. The essence of the service was the same. However, the assembly stood at prayers and sat when it sang; and stood when it sang and knelt at prayer at times. There was no specified liturgy in any of the Kirks. I've gone to a Free Kirk that didn't have a pulpit; the pastor stood on an elevated platform, like a speaker in a lecture hall, but such practice is unnecessary. If I'm not mistaken, the Kirks have several collections of hymns, which were formerly regarded as 'things of human fabrication,' and so 'idolatrous.' However, hymns, as well as organs, harmoniums, and other musical instruments, are now in use. As a result, the Kirks' faces are similar and sisterly:

There is no such thing as an all-encompassing face. There are no exceptions, no matter how many decent esse fora.

What is the difference between the Free Church, the Established Church, and the United Presbyterian Church, the Southron used to wonder? If the Southron posed the question to a Scottish acquaintance, the Scottish friend was unlikely to respond. He may be a member of Scotland's 'Episcopal' community, but he's just as uneducated as any Anglican. Or he may not have done these significant studies in Scottish history, which shed light on this enigmatic topic.

Indeed, the whole nature of the enigma has recently transformed, much like the colors in a kaleidoscope. The most prominent colors are no longer 'Auld Kirk,' 'Free Kirk,' and 'U.P.'s,' but 'Auld Kirk,' 'Free Kirk,' and 'United Free Kirk.' The United Free Kirk was formed in 1900 from the ancient 'United Presbyterians' (as old as 1847), with an overwhelming majority of the old Free Kirk, while the Free Kirk of today is made up of a minuscule minority of the old Free Kirk. The latter refused to join the recent merger. The Free Kirk, colloquially known as 'The Wee Frees,' now has the riches that the old Free Kirk's before, in 1900, combined with the United Presbyterians. Thanks to a verdict, it formed the United Free Church (one may easily call it a 'judgment') of the House of Lords (August 1, 1904). It is anticipated that common sense would find an 'out gait,' or issue, from this unpleasant situation. 'Those who are at all receptive to a sense of national dishonor look forward gladly to such a prospect; they have been spectators already too long to the struggle that has separated our tiny corner of Christendom,' said Mr. R.L. Stevenson, then a sage of twenty-four, in 1874. According to R.L.S., the perennial schisms of the Kirk show "something pathetic for the sorrowful man, but painfully amusing for others."

The irony of the current situation is palpable. About half of the Kirk of Scotland ministers deserted their mansions and nice glebes two generations ago for the sake of certain principles. Unfortunately, they abandoned some of these notions or left them in suspense a few years ago, and as a consequence, they have lost, if only for the time being, their manses, stipends, colleges, and attractive glebes.

Why should all of this be the case? The explanation can only be found in the history of the Scottish Reformation, which is both sorrowful and painfully hilarious. When John Knox died on November 24, 1572, a good burgess of Edinburgh wrote in his Diary, 'John Knox, minister, dying, who had, as was said, the most of the blame of all the sufferings of Scotland, since the massacre of the late Cardinal,' Beaton, assassinated at St. Andrews in 1546. Three hundred thirty-two years have passed since his death, and the current woes of the United Free Kirk are direct if the distant outcome of some of John Knox's beliefs.

The whole problem stems from his unusual ideas regarding the relationship between Church and State and his followers. In 1843, half of the ministers of the Established Kirk in Scotland, if not more, left the Kirk and headed into the wilderness in search of what they saw as Knox's ideal. They face a similar exodus in 1904 because they are no longer steadfast supporters of the same goal! Nevertheless, a small minority of around twenty-seven pastors sticks to the Knoxian ideal. All the money lavished to the Free Kirk by devout patrons over the last sixty years is rewarded by all the money lavished to the Free Kirk.

For 344 years (1560-1904), the fight has been about Church-State ties, as we know. According to Lord Macnaghten, who offered one of the two views in favor of the United Free Kirk's claim to the property held by the Free Kirk before its merger with the United Presbyterians in 1900, the rupture of 1843 developed as a result of the Free Kirk's withdrawal from the Established Kirk. According to the sympathetic judge, there were two groups in the Established Church before 1843: the 'Moderates' and the 'Evangelicals' (also known as 'The Wild Men,' 'the Highland Host,' or 'High Flyers'). The Evangelicals gained the majority, and they ruled with a heavy fist. They enacted Acts in the Assembly that were entirely beyond the power of a legally founded Church... The State refused to acknowledge their allegations. The strong arm of the law curtailed their excesses. They still held that their actions were authorized and necessary by the teaching of Christ's Headship, to which they ascribed particular and exceptional importance.'

Now, between 1838-1843, the State could not and would not allow these 'extravagances' in a State-paid Church. As a result, the Evangelical party seceded, claiming that "we are still the Church of Scotland, the only Church that deserves the name, the only Church that can be known and recognized by the maintaining of those principles to which the Church of our fathers was true when she was on the mountain and the field when she was under persecution when she was an outcast."

Thus, the Free Kirk was the Kirk, whereas the Established

Kirk was heretical, or as Knox would have put it, 'ane rotten Laodicean.' The Church of Scotland had been a Kirk established by law (or by what was said to be a legal Parliament) since August 1560, but had never, perhaps, for an hour attained its full ideal relation to the State; had never been granted its entire claims, but only so much or so little of these as the political situation compelled the State to concede, or enabled it to withdraw. There had always been Kirk members who claimed all that the Free Kirk demanded in 1843, but they never obtained nearly as much as they demanded; they frequently received much less than they desired, and no State could provide the whole amount of their aspirations to a State-paid Church. Only by separating the Church from the State could total independence be achieved. The Free Kirk broke away, but they maintained that they were the Church of Scotland and that the State had a responsibility to create and sustain them while providing them complete freedom.

In 1851, an Act and Declaration of the Free Kirk's Assembly stated: 'She holds still, and through God's grace will ever hold, that civil ruler must recognize the truth of God according to His word, and to promote and support the Kingdom of Christ without assuming any jurisdiction in it, or any power over it....'

If we may speak carnally, the state should pay the piper but not pretend to set the music.

Now we're getting close to the mystery: what was the difference between the Free Kirk and the United Presbyterians, who have been merged with that organization since 1900? The disagreement was that the Free Kirk believed it was the State's responsibility to create her and leave her in complete independence. Still, the United Presbyterians held the polar opposite view: the State cannot and must not create any Church or fund any Church out of national resources. So when the two Kirks merged in 1900, the Free Kirk either abandoned the belief about which she claimed in 1851 that "she maintains it yet, and by God's grace ever shall maintain it," or she saw it as a mere pious view that did not prohibit her from joining a Kirk with opposite principles. The small minority—the Wee Frees, today's Free Kirk—would not accept this compromise, 'therefore these tears,' to hide disagreements in fundamentally metaphysical doctrine.

Now, as we have indicated, the foundation of all the problems, all the schisms, and sorrows of more than three centuries resides in some of John Knox's beliefs, and one wonders what Kirk John Knox would be if he were living today. I believe the venerable Reformer would be found among the ranks of the Established Kirk, or 'the Auld Kirk.' He would not have gone into the wilderness in 1843, and he would have disagreed with the United Presbyterians' ideals. This notion may seem surprising at first look, but it was developed after many hours of careful thought.

To the extent that he ever reasoned them out, Knox's theories rested on this unassailable rock, namely, that Calvinism, as he regarded it, was definite in every detail. If the State, or "the civil magistrate," as he called it, agreed with

Knox, Knox was thrilled that the State should control religion. As it was in John Knox, the magistrate was to bring down Catholicism and other deviations from the truth with every possible tool of the law, including physical punishment, jail, exile, and death. If the State was ready and prepared to accomplish all of this, it was to be fully followed in religious issues. The authority in its hands was God-given—in reality, the State was the secular element of the Church. In this idealized view of the State, Knox talks on the magistrate's religious allegiance, in the style of what would be dubbed the strongest 'Erastianism' in this nation. The State 'rules the roast' in all things of religion and may, as Laud and Charles I., attempted, modify modes of worship—but only if the State completely agrees with the Kirk.

Thus, under Edward VI, Knox would have wished for the secular authority in England, the civil judge, to ban people from kneeling during the Sacrament's performance. That was perfectly within the State's jurisdiction, simply and only because Knox did not want people to kneel. However, when the civil judge insisted on people kneeling in Scotland long after Knox's death, supporters of Knox's principles disagreed that the judge (James VI.) had the jurisdiction to give such an order, and many refused to follow while staying inside the Established Church. They did not 'disrupt,' as the Free Church did; they just did what they liked and branded their loyal brothers as 'illegal pastors.' The eventual result was that they sparked the Civil War, with the famous Jenny Geddes firing the first shot, hurling her stool at the reader at St. Giles'. Thus, the

State was to be followed in issues of religion only when the State performed Kirk's bidding, and not otherwise. When he was originally hired as a 'licensed preacher' and State agent in England, Knox accepted as much of the State's liturgy as he chose; when the ritual required the people to kneel, Knox and his Berwick congregation resisted. He and the other royal priests, speaking before the King at Easter, condemned his ministers, Northumberland and the others, with equal openness. In his speech, Knox referred to them as Judas, Shebna, and other biblical villains. Later, he apologized for putting things so lightly; he should have addressed the ministers by their names, not cloaked things in a suggestion. In a sermon spoken before her, we cannot readily imagine a chaplain of her late Majesty, condemning the Chancellor of the Exchequer as 'Judas,' remark Mr. Gladstone. Nonetheless, Knox, a licensed preacher of a State Church, indulged his spiritual freedom' to that amount and felt ashamed that he had not gone further.

If this is 'Erastianism,' it is of a peculiar kind. Knox's opinion is that in a Catholic state, the ruler is not to be followed in religious issues by sincere believers; Knox said that the Catholic ruler should face 'passive opposition .' At other times, he should be murdered at sight. Over eighteen months, he expressed these many theories. In a Protestant nation, Catholics must follow the Protestant monarch or face imprisonment, exile, burning, and death. In a Protestant State, the Protestant monarch is to be followed in spiritual issues by Protestants. The extent that Kirk approves of his actions, or even further, in practice, if there is no likelihood of effective opposition.

If he had been living and still held his old principles in 1843, we may assume that Knox would not have left the Established Church for the Free Church since he did consent to numerous State rules that he did not approve of at the time. For example, he did not approve of bishops, and the Kirk created on his model in 1560 had no bishops. But, twelve years later, the State reintroduced bishops in the figure of the ruffian Regent Morton, and Knox did not withdraw to 'the mountain and the fields,' but made the most practical efforts to get the best conditions for the Kirk. He was elderly and worn out, yet he stayed in the Established Kirk and counseled no one to leave.

Again, as it was the Free Kirk's, it was his view that there should be no 'patronage,' no presenting ministers to cures by the patron. The congregations were to pick and 'call' any suitably qualified individual at their leisure, as they do today in all Kirks, including the Established Church (from 1874). However, throughout Knox's lifetime, the State overruled the Church's prerogative. Archibald Douglas, the most notorious criminal of the age, was given to the Kirk of Glasgow. The lords made numerous similar presents of evil and stupid cadets to prestigious livings. Morton made one of Riccio's killers a bishop! However, Knox did not advocate secession; rather, he suggested that non-residence, scandalous conduct, or erroneous theology on the part of the person submitted render his proposal 'invalid and of no force or effect, and this to take place likewise in the selection of the bishops.' As a result, Knox was a bit of an opportunist at times. If he had been living in 1843, he would have stayed in the Establishment and pushed to eliminate 'patronage,' which was achieved from inside in 1874. If this theory is correct, the Free Kirk was more Knoxian than John Knox and deviated from his norm. He was willing to give up a lot of spiritual independence' rather than split with the State. Many times, long after he died, the National Church, under duress, accepted concessions.

Knox understood the distinction between the ideal and the practical. It was ideal for all non-convertible Catholics to "die the death." But the ideal was never realized because the State was unwilling to assist the Kirk in this subject. It was perfect for any of 'the brothers,' aware of a vocation and sensing an opportunity, to treat an impenitent Catholic monarch as Jehu handled Jezebel. However, if any of the brothers had contacted Knox about the legality of assassinating Queen Mary in 1561-67, he would have discovered his error. He would have down the Reformer's steps far faster than he had climbed them.

Nonetheless, despite his willingness to compromise, Knox had a wonderfully mystical conception of the Kirk and its clergy. In his preface to The Judgment of the House of Lords, the editor of The Free Church Union Case, Mr. Taylor Innes (himself the author of a biography of the Reformer), writes: 'The Church of Scotland, as a Protestant Church, had its origin in the year 1560, for its first Confession dates from August and its first Assembly from December in that year.' In actuality, the Confession was recognized and approved as law in August 1560 by a very shaky legal Convention of the Estates. But Knox believed that the Protestant Church in, if not of, Scotland existed a year before that day and held 'the Keys' authority and, it would seem, 'the power of the Sword' before that day. The Protestant Church was 'a Church in existence' as soon as a local group of men of his views convened and picked a pastor and preacher who also administered the Sacraments. The Catholic Church, which had been formed by law at the time, was, according to Knox, no Church at all; her priests were not 'lawful ministers,' her Pope was the man of Sin ex officio, and the Church was 'the Kirk of the malignants'—'a lady of pleasure reared in Babylon.'

On the other hand, the true Church—even if it was just 200 men—was challenging the Kirk of the malignants, and it was the only one who was genuine. The State did not create and could not undo "the Trew Church," but it was obligated to build, develop, and obey it.

From 1559 until 1690, this final clause precipitated 130 years of violence, 'persecution,' and general discontent in Scotland. Why did the Kirk spend so much time 'in the heather,' hunting like a partridge on the field and the mountain? When Kirk's wilder spirits were not being persecuted, they were persecuting the State and tormenting the individual subject. All of this stemmed from Knox's conception of the Church. A small group of Calvinistic Protestants and a 'lawful preacher' were all that was required to form a Church. At first, little more than a 'call' to a preacher from a local group of Calvinistic Protestants was necessary to form a valid minister (eventually, significantly more was necessary). However, once the 'call' was granted and accepted, the notion held that the 'lawful minister' was superior to the State's rules as the legendary emperor was to grammar. A few 'lawful ministers' of this type possessed 'the power of the Keys;' they could excommunicate anyone and hand them over to Satan, and (apparently) they could present 'the power of the Sword' to any town council, which could then decree capital punishment against any Catholic priest who celebrated Mass, as he was required to do by State law. Knox's Kirk's moderate and fair requests in May 1559, before the Convention of Estates, ratified it in August 1560. It was because the wilder spirits among the pastors, rather than the Church, persisted in these assertions that the State, when given the opportunity, drove them into moors and mosses and hung quite a number of them.

I have never seen these circumstances completely described by any historian or biographer of Knox, save by the Reformer himself, partially in his History and partially in letters to a woman he knew. The riddle of the Kirks revolves around Knox's definition of the 'lawful minister' and his claim to absolute power.

To offer an example, Knox himself was a 'priest of the altar,' 'one of Baal's shaved type,' between 1540 and 1543. He then claimed nothing on that score. Following the assassination of Cardinal Beaton, the killers and their followers formed a congregation in the Castle of St. Andrews and asked Knox to be their preacher. He was now a 'legitimate minister.' In May 1559, he and four or five similarly legal pastors, two of whom were converted friars, one of whom was a baker, and one, Harlow, a tailor, joined forces with their Protestant supporters to burn the monasteries in Perth, as well as the altars and decorations of the church there. They immediately claimed 'the Keys' authority and threatened to excommunicate any friends who did not join them in arms. They, 'the brotherhood,' also opposed the death penalty for any priest who said Mass in Perth. The legitimate ministers could no longer contemplate hanging the priests themselves. They must have put 'the authority of the Sword' on the bellies and town council of Perth, I believe, since the Regent, Mary of Guise, removed these men from office when she invaded the town, which was considered as an illegal and perfidious move on her side. Again, in the summer of 1560, when Catholicism was still legal, the bellies of Edinburgh condemned the death sentence for obstinate Catholics. The Kirk also assigned legitimate pastors to some of the larger cities, establishing herself before the Estates recognized her in August 1560. Nothing could be more free and absolute than the Kirk in her early stages. On the other hand, even during Knox's lifetime, the State, having the upper hand under the Regent Morton, a strong man, introduced a modified kind of prelacy and patronage; did not restore to the Kirk her ' inheritance,'—the lands of the old

Church; and only hanged one priest, not improbably for a personal reason.

Thus, from the start, there was a conflict between the Protestant Church and the State. At different times, one preacher is believed to have stated that he was the lone 'lawful minister' in Scotland; and one of these persons, Mr. Cargill, excommunicated Charles II., while another, Mr Renwick, launched an assassination campaign against the Government. Both males were executed by hanging.

These were extreme claims of spiritual independence,' and the Kirk, or at least the majority of preachers, objected to such behavior, which may have been the logical extension of the idea of the 'lawful minister,' but was exceedingly uncomfortable in practice. Nevertheless, Kirk as a whole was devoted.

Sometimes the State, led by a powerful leader like Morton or James Stewart, Earl of Arran (a thoroughpaced ruffian), crushed the Church's pretensions. At times, as when Andrew Melville headed the Kirk under James VI., she asserted that there was only one monarch in Scotland, Christ and that the real King, the kid, James VI., was nothing more than 'Christ's stupid vassal.' In earthly affairs, he was paramount, but the Church's judicature was superior in spiritual things.

This seems to be completely reasonable, but who was to define what things were spiritual and which were temporal? The Kirk asserted the power to determine that matter; thus, it could spiritualize any issue of statesmanship, such as a royal marriage, commerce with Catholic Spain, which the Kirk prohibited, or the expulsion of Catholic peers. 'There is a judgment above yours, and that is God's; place it in the hands of the ministers, for we will judge the angels, said the apostle,' said the Rev. Mr. Pont to James VI. 'Ye shall sit upon twelve thrones and judge,' says Mr. Pont, referring to the apostles and, by extension, ministers.

In 1596, everything came to a head. The King asked officials of the Kirk if he might bring back certain earls who had been exiled for being Catholics provided they satisfied the Kirk.' He may not, according to the response. Knox had long argued that "a prophet" might teach treason (he is pretty specific about this) and that the prophet, as well as whoever carried out his teaching, would be innocent. At the time, a preacher was accused of preaching slanderously, and he refused to be tried by anybody other than his peers. What Court of Appeal could overturn the judgment of men who professed to 'judge angels' if they acquitted him, as they were morally guaranteed to do? A riot erupted in Edinburgh, and the King took his moment, gripped his nettle, the civic authorities supported him, and, in practice, the demands of real ministers provided little problem from then on until the foolishness of Charles I. led to the establishment of the Covenant. The Sovereign had overreached his powers as outrageously as the Kirk had, and the consequence was that the Kirk, now with the nobility and the people in arms on her side, was completely autocratic for roughly twelve years. Her crowning accomplishment was to successfully oppose the Estates in Parliament, leaving Scotland exposed to Cromwellian occupation. Noll accomplished what the Plantagenets and Tudors could not: he seized Scotland after the Kirk had paralyzed the State. The preachers discovered Cromwell to be a perfect 'Malignant,' refusing to allow prophets to preach treason or even let the General Assembly gathering. They could judge angels but not Ironsides; ex-communication and 'Kirk discipline' were frowned upon, and witches were seldom burnt. Cromwell said that the preachers 'had done their duty,' having discharged their bolt.

At this point, they broke into two factions: the Extremists, who referred to themselves as "the divine," and the men of a softer disposition.

During the Restoration, Charles II. should have sided with the softer group, some of whom were eager to have their ferocious colleagues exiled to Orkney, out of the way. But Charles's slogan was 'Never again .' He reinstated bishops without the despised liturgy via a pettifogging farce. After years of risings and suppressions, the ministers were forced to submit, receiving an 'indulgence' from the State. At the same time, only a few defenders of the clergy's ancient pretensions remained in the wildernesses of Southwestern Scotland. There may be three or four such ministers, or just one, but they, or he, were the only 'lawful ministers' in the eyes of 'the Remnant.' During the Revolution of 1688-89, the Remnant refused to accept the agreement that resulted in the re-establishment of the Presbyterian Kirk. They stood out, splintering into several sects; in 1847, the spiritual successors of the majority of them merged into a single organization known as 'The United Presbyterian Kirk.' The Moderates were in the majority in the Established Church until around 1837, when the inheritors of Knox's severe beliefs, which the majority of clergy rejected before the Revolution of 1688, gained the upper hand. They had placed their sort of ministers in the Highlands' most distant parishes, who drowned the votes of the Lowland Moderates in 1838, just as Highland 'Moderates' had drowned the votes of the Lowland Extremists under James VI. In 1843, most Extremists, or most of them, left the Kirk and formed the Free Kirk. When the Free Kirk joined the United Presbyterians in 1900, it was mostly Highland preachers who refused to accept the new union and today compose the true Free Kirk, or Wee Frees, with the endowments of the ancient Free Kirk of 1843. We can hardly say Beati possessors.

It has been shown, or I have attempted, erroneously or not, to show that, as wild and impossible as Knox's, Andrew Melville's, Mr. Pont's, and others' outstanding claims were, the old Scottish Kirk of 1560, by law established, was capable of giving up or suppressing these claims, even under Knox, and even while the Covenant remained in force. The majority of ministers were not irreconcilables after Charles II's return, before the Worcester war, before terrible Dunbar. By historical continuity, the Auld Kirk, the Kirk Established, has some right to call herself the Church of Scotland. In contrast, the opposing claimants, the men of 1843, appear to be descended from people like young Renwick, the last hero who died for their ideas, but not the only 'lawful minister' between Tweed and Cape Wrath. Other times, other methods.' All the Kirks are perfectly loyal; now none persecutes; interference with private life, 'Kirk discipline,' is at an all-time low; and, but for this recent 'parboil,' as our old writers put it, we might have said that, despite differences in terminology, all the Kirks are finally united in the only union worth having, that of peace and goodwill. That connection, let us hope, may be restored by good temper and common reason, traits that have not hitherto been prominent in the religious history of Scotland or England.

THE CONSPIRACY OF GOWRIE

The bizarre events known as 'The Gowrie Conspiracy' or 'The Slaying of the Ruthvens' unfolded in the following way, based on evidence that no one denies. On August 5, 1600, the King, James VI., left the stables at the House of Falkland to shoot a deer when the Master of Ruthven rode up and asked the king a question. Then, around seven o'clock in the morning, something happened. The Master was nineteen years old and lived with his brother, the Earl of Gowrie, who was twenty-two, in the family townhome in Perth, some twelve or fourteen miles from Falkland. After the conversation, the King pursued the hounds, and the 'long and painful' pursuit culminated in a kill near Falkland at around eleven o'clock. The King and the Master then rode to Perth, accompanied by around fifteen members of the Royal escort, including the Duke of Lennox and the Earl of Mar. Others from the King's company joined them; the total number may have been as few as twenty-five.

When they arrived in Perth, it seemed that they had not been anticipated. The Earl having eaten at noon, the Royal supper was delayed until two o'clock, and after the meager meal, the King and Master went upstairs alone. In contrast, the Earl of Gowrie led Lennox and others into his garden at the rear of the house, bordering on the Tay. While they were eating cherries, a Gowrie servant, Thomas Cranstoun (brother of Sir John of that ilk), received word that the King had already mounted and galloped out through the Inch of Perth. Gowrie requested horses, but Cranstoun informed him that his horses were two miles away in Scone, over the Tay. The gentlemen then walked to the house's street entrance, where the keeper informed them that the King had not ridden away. Gowrie lied to him, re-entered the home, went upstairs, and returned to persuade Lennox that James had left. All of this is proven on the stand by Lennox, Mar, Lindores, and a slew of other witnesses.

While the group remained outside the gate, a tower window above them opened, and the King emerged, angry, yelling 'Treason!' and pleading with Mar for assistance. Mar, along with Lennox and the majority of the others, rushed to the rescue up the home's main staircase, where they were met with a closed door that they couldn't open. Gowrie had not gone with his guests to help the King; instead, he was waiting in the street, wondering, 'What is the matter?' When two members of the King's household, Thomas and James Erskine, sought to capture him, the 'treason was committed beneath Gowrie's own home. His companions drove the Erskines away, and several Murrays from Tullibardine who were in Perth for a wedding encircled him. Gowrie fled, pulled a pair of 'twin swords,' and made his way inside his house's courtyard, joined by Cranstoun and others. They discovered the corpse of a guy lying at the foot of a short dark stairway, either injured or dead. Cranstoun dashed up the dimly lit stairwell, followed by Gowrie, two Ruthvens, Hew Moncrieff, Patrick Eliot, and maybe more. They discovered Sir Thomas Erskine, a crippled Dr. Herries, a young gentleman of the Royal Household named

John Ramsay, and Wilson, a servant, with drawn swords at the top of the short spiral stair. Cranstoun was injured, and he and his comrades left, abandoning Gowrie, who had been run through the body by Ramsay. All the time, the other door of the long Gallery Chamber rang with the hammer blows of Lennox and his crew while the town bell summoned the residents. Erskine and Ramsay had now shut the door opening on the tiny stairwell, which the retainers of Gowrie had hit with axes. The King's party forced the lock and entered Lennox, Mar, and the rest of the King's entourage by using a hamper delivered to them through a hole in the other door of the gallery. They allowed James out of a tiny turret opening from the Gallery Chamber, and after some disputes with the enraged mob and Perth's magistrates, they took the King to Falkland after dark.

The end consequence was the deaths of Gowrie and his brother, the Master (whose corpse was found at the bottom of the tiny stairway), as well as Ramsay, Dr. Herries, and several of Gowrie's retainers.

The killing of the Master of Ruthven was described as follows: "When James yelled 'Treason!' from the stable door, young Ramsay heard his voice but not his words." He'd hurried into the quadrangle, dashed up the tight steps, discovered a door behind which a fight could be heard, 'dang in' the door, and seen the King battling with the Master. Behind them stood a guy, the center of the enigma, to which he paid no attention. Instead, he drew his sword, cut the Master across the face and neck, and shoved him downstairs. Ramsay immediately appealed to Sir Thomas Erskine from the window, who, together with Herries and Wilson, rushed to his aid, murdered the injured Master, and imprisoned James (who had no weapon) in the turret. Then there was the battle in which Gowrie died. Except for a townsman who subsequently retracted his testimony, no one saw the mystery man on the tower again.

The entire thing was observed by the King's troops, the retainers of Gowrie, and several Perth civilians. There was no trace of Gowrie and his party's scheme or scheme. His supporters claimed that he intended to depart Perth that day for 'Lothian,' that is, for his castle at Dirleton, near North Berwick, where he had despatched most of his soldiers and foodstuffs. They stated James had asked the Master to meet him at Falkland, and Gowrie had never expected the Master to return with the King.

James's version was given in a public letter written to the King's dictation at Falkland by David Moysie, a notary, on the night of the events, which we only know about through the report of Nicholson, the English resident at Holyrood (August 6). Nicholson only repeated what Elphinstone, the secretary, told him about the contents of the letter, written to the King's dictation at Falkland by David Moysie, a not At the end of August, James prepared and distributed a detailed narrative that was almost similar to Nicholson's account of Elphinstone's description on the contents of the August 5

Falkland letter.

The King's story is widely believed until we get to the point when he talks with Alexander Ruthven in Falkland before the buck-hunt begins. There was such an interview, which lasted approximately a quarter of an hour, but only James understood what it was about. He claims that after an exceptionally low obeisance, Ruthven told him the following story:—While walking alone in the meadows outside Perth the previous evening, he saw 'a base-like guy, unknown to him, with a cloak, draped around his lips,' a standard measure to prevent identification. When asked who he was and what his mission was 'in such a lonesome region, being remote from all means,' the man was taken aback. Ruthven apprehended him and discovered "a large, broad pot, all full of coined gold in huge bits" under his arm. Ruthven transported the guy to Perth and put him in a 'privy darned house'—that is, a room—while keeping the secret to himself. He left Perth at 4 a.m. to inform the King, encouraging him to 'take order' in the situation immediately since Lord Gowrie was unaware of it. When James argued it was none of his concern since the gold was not a treasure trove, Ruthven labeled him 'too scrupulous,' adding that his brother, Gowrie, 'and other important men,' may intervene. James then inquired about the money and their bearer, assuming that the gold was foreign, smuggled in by Jesuits for Catholic insurgents. Ruthven responded that the bearer seemed to be a previously unknown 'Scots guy' and that the gold seemed foreign mintage. As a result, James was convinced that the gold was foreign, and the carrier disguised Scots priest. As a result, he recommended sending back with Ruthven a retainer of his own, accompanied by a warrant to Gowrie, then Provost of Perth, and the Bailies, to seize the man and the money. Ruthven said that if they did, the money would be wasted and pleaded with the King to ride over immediately, be 'the first seer,' and award him 'at his honorable discretion.'

The weirdness of the story and the weirdness of Ruthven's demeanor astounded James, who answered that he would respond after the search was ended. Ruthven speculated that the guy would make a disturbance and uncover the entire thing, leading the riches to be tampered with. Gowrie would miss him, yet Gowrie and the townspeople would be 'at the preaching if James arrived immediately.' James remained silent and followed the dogs. Still, he meditated on the narrative, and he was summoned.

Ruthven and promised to accompany him to Perth soon after the quest was over.

In this section, James explains that, though he was unaware that any man was with Ruthven, he did have two friends, one of whom, Andrew Henderson, now sent to Gowrie, instructing him to prepare supper for the King. This is not direct proof from James. He was unaware and unconcerned that any guy alive had arrived with Ruthven.

Ruthven was constantly close to the King throughout the pursuit, pressing him to 'hurry the finish of the hunting.' The buck was killed near the stables, and Ruthven refused to let James wait for a second horse: dispatched after him. So the king didn't even linger to 'brittle' the deer, instead of informing the Duke of Lennox, Mar, and others that he was riding to Perth to consult with Gowrie and would return before sunset. Some of the Court proceeded to Falkland to get new horses, while others followed slowly with tired steeds. They followed 'unwanted by him,' since there was the word that the King was about to seize the harsh Master of Oliphant. Ruthven pleaded with James not to send Lennox and Mar, but merely three or four slaves, to which the King replied: "half furiously."

James was suspicious of this unusual behavior. He'd known Ruthven, who was vying for the position of Gentleman of the Bedchamber, or Cubicular. 'The furthest that the King's suspicion could go was, that it may be that the Earl, his brother, had treated him so harshly that the young gentleman, being of a high spirit, had taken such displeasure that he was over himself;' hence his strange, disturbed, and melancholy behavior. While they were riding, James checked his phone.

Lennox, whose first wife was Gowrie's sister. Lennox had never seen anything like mental instability in young Ruthven. Still, James ordered the Duke to 'accompanies him into that dwelling' (chamber), where the money and its carrier lay. Lennox believed the gold tale was 'unlikely.' Ruthven, observing them conversing, advised James to be discreet and bring no one with him to the initial examination of the riches.

As a result, the King rode onward 'between trust and mistrust.' Ruthven sent his second friend, Andrew Ruthven, to Gowrie about two miles from Perth. Ruthven galloped ahead of the rest of the party when they were within a mile of Perth. Gowrie was at supper, having ignored the two previous messengers.

Gowrie met James 'near the end of the Inch,' with fifty or sixty men; the Royal entourage was then of fifteen people, with swords only, and no daggers or 'whingers.' Dinner did not materialize for another hour (say 2 p.m.). James whispered to Ruthven that he needed to view the riches right now; Ruthven advised him to wait and not attract Gowrie's suspicions by whispering ('rounding'). As a result, James focused his chat on Gowrie, receiving "only half words and poor phrases" from him. ' When it was time for dinner, Gowrie stood pensively beside the King's table, frequently talking to the servants, 'and oft-times walked in and out,' as he did before supper. The suite waited about, as was customary until James was ready to eat when Gowrie brought them to their separate table in the hall; 'he sat not down with them as the normal fashion is,' but remained quietly by the King, who bantered him 'in a homely fashion.'

Having sat for too long, Ruthven murmured to James that he longed to be free of him.

Because Ruthven had requested it, James dispatched Gowrie into the hall to present a type of grace-cup to the suite, as was customary. James then stood to join Ruthven, requesting that Sir Thomas Erskine accompany him. Ruthven urged that James 'order openly' that no one follows at once, pledging that 'he should make anyone or two follow that he liked to call for.'

The King then proceeded alone with Ruthven past the end of the hall, up a staircase, and past three or four apartments, Ruthven 'ever shutting behind him every door as he went,' anticipating attendants who never arrived since Ruthven never requested them. We don't know if James saw the doors lock or deduced it from the subsequent revelation that one door was locked. Then Ruthven presented a more cheerful smile than he had all day, always stating that he had him sure and secure enough guarded. ' Finally, they arrived at 'a tiny study' (a turret room), where James discovered 'not a bondman, but a freeman, with a dagger at his waist and a most abased visage.' Ruthven shut the turret door, pulled the man's dagger, and pointed it at the King's breast, 'avowing now that the King behooved to be in his will and used as the list,' threatening death if James shouted out or opened the window. He also reminded the King of the loss of his father, the late Gowrie (executed for treason in 1584). In a while, the other guy was 'trembling and quaking.' James launched into a lengthy rant on various topics, vowing forgiveness and quiet provided Ruthven immediately let him go. Ruthven then revealed the truth and assured James that his life would be securely provided he remained silent; the rest Gowrie would explain. Then, instructing the other guy to guard the King, he left, closing the door behind him. He'd made James vow not to open the window. In his short absence, James learned from the armed guy that he had just lately been locked up in the turret for reasons he didn't understand. James told him to open the window with his 'right hand.' The guy did what he was told.

The King's narration reverts to a subject outside of his perception here (the events which occurred downstairs during his absence). Many aristocrats and gentlemen have sworn under oath to substantiate his story. He claims (and we repeat what we said before) that, while he was absent, as his train was rising from supper, one of the Earl's servants, Cranstoun, hurried in swiftly, telling the Earl that the King had gotten on a horse, and 'was going across the Inch' (isle) of Perth. The Earl informed the nobility, and they all went to the gate. The porter reassured them that the King had not left the palace. Gowrie told the porter a falsehood but then turned to Lennox and Mar and claimed he'd obtain further information. He then raced back across the court and upstairs, returning hurriedly with the news that 'the King had gone, long ago, via the rear gate, and would not be overtaken unless they hastened.'

On their way to the stables for their horses, the aristocrats had to pass through the tower's window on the first level, where James was imprisoned. Ruthven had returned at this point, 'throwing his hands about in a frenzied fashion as a man lost.' He then sought to tie the royal hands with his garter, declaring no remedy for it and that the King had to die. During the battle, James dragged Ruthven towards the previously open window. When the King's companions were waiting on the street below, with Gowrie among them, James yelled for aid, 'holding out the right side of his head and his right elbow.' Gowrie stood 'always wondering what it meant,' but as we saw, Lennox, Mar, and others rushed in and up the main staircase to locate the King.

Meanwhile, James forced Ruthven out of the tower, 'the said Mr. Alexander's head under his arms, and himself on his knees,' towards the room door that led to the dark stairway. 'The other gentleman is doing nothing but standing behind the King's back and shivering all the while,' James was attempting to gain hold of Ruthven's sword and draw it. A young gentleman of the Royal Household, John Ramsay, arrived from the dark rear staircase at this time and struck Ruthven with his knife. 'The other guy backed out. James then forced Ruthven down the rear steps, where he was killed by Sir Thomas Erskine and Dr. Herries, who were approaching from that direction. The remainder of the story began with Gowrie's death. James's return to Falkland was delayed for two or three hours due to a riot among the townspeople.

This is the published version of the King's story. It corresponds closely with the letter sent to Cecil by Nicholson, the English agent, on August 6.

On August 5, James had his version, from which he never deviated, ready. Only one conclusion can be taken from his story. Gowrie and his brother had attempted to get James to their home when he was practically unsupervised. They had an armed guy on the turret who would help the Master grab the King. The scheme was thwarted when James was well attended, the armed man turned coward, and Gowrie falsely declared the King's departure to have his entourage follow back to Falkland and so leave the King in the hands of his captors. The conspiracy could not be abandoned after it was planned since the plotters had no prisoner with a pot of money to deliver. Thus their intended treason would have been obvious.

How well does James' story hold up? At the Ruthvens' postmortem trial in November, witnesses such as Lennox testified to a quarter-hour conversation with Ruthven at Falkland before the hunt. The early arrival of Andrew Henderson to Gowrie's residence, at half-past ten, is attested to by two gentlemen called Hay and one called Moncrieff, who was then with Gowrie on business, to which he immediately refused to attend further, in the case of the Hays. A manuscript vindication of the Ruthvens further supports Henderson's attendance in Falkland released at the time. None of the King's party saw him, and their failure to testify that they did see him demonstrates their honesty. Thus, Gowrie arranged no supper for the King, despite Henderson's early arrival with word of his impending visit, demonstrating that Gowrie intended to seem surprised. Again, Henderson's travel on the night of August 5 demonstrates that he was involved: why else would a guy travel who had not been seen by anybody (save a Perth witness who retracted his testimony) connected with the terrible events? Except for a few of Gowrie's retainers who actively participated in the conflict, no one else escaped.

The Kingside with Ruthven in a dispute over ownership of the church lands of Scone, which Gowrie owned and Ruthven coveted, explains James' notion that Ruthven was crazy as a result of brutal treatment by his brother Gowrie. This is referenced lightly in a current document. [13] Again, Lennox testified under oath that James told him the tale of the lure, the pot of gold, as they rode to Perth. Lennox was an honorable guy who had married Gowrie's sister.

On his way back to Gowrie's home, Ruthven informed a retainer, Craigingelt, that he'd been on an errand not far distant,' and explained the King's appearance by claiming he'd been 'brought' by the royal saddler to collect payment of a debt to the man. However, now that James has granted Gowrie a year's protection from creditor pursuit, there is no evidence of the saddler's presence. Ruthven had lied to Craigingelt; he had been at Falkland, not 'on an errand not far away.'

Cranstoun, Gowrie's man, confirmed bringing the news, or rumor, of the King's departure. On oath, Lennox, Lindores, Ray (a magistrate of Perth), the porter himself, and others established that Gowrie went inside the house to check the truth; urged that it was real; spoke the lie to the porter, who denied it; and sought to have the King's company take a horse and follow.

The fact that the King was trapped behind a door that

couldn't be broken open is undeniable.

All of these are facts that cannot be denied. However, they were called into question when Henderson, Gowrie's factor or steward and a Perth town councilor, emerged from hiding between August 11 and August 20, narrated his tale, and admitted to being the man on the turret. On the night of August 4, he said that Gowrie ordered him to ride to Falkland with the Master of Ruthven and return with any message that Ruthven may convey. When the Hays and Moncrieff spotted him, he returned with word that the King was on his way. An hour later, Gowrie told him to put on a mail shirt and plate sleeves because he would arrest a Highlander in the Shoe-gait. Later, when the King arrived, Henderson was sent to Ruthven in the gallery and ordered to perform whatever was requested. Ruthven then locked him up in the turret without explaining why. The King was eventually taken inside the turret, and Henderson claims that, to a little measure, he calmed Ruthven's fury. During Ramsay and Ruthven's fight, he crept downstairs, went home, and escaped that night.

Henderson's presence at Falkland was disputed at all. Nobody attested to his being there, but it is acknowledged by the modern apologist, who accuses the King of organizing the whole plot against the Ruthvens. Even though the courtyard was full, no one saw Henderson slink away from the tight stairwell. However, one Robertson, a Perth notary, testified (September 23) that he saw Henderson slip out of the tiny stairway and walk over the Master's corpse; Robertson called to him, but he did not respond. If Robertson lied on September 23, he withdrew, or rather, withheld, his testimony during the November trial. If he had stuck to his earlier declaration, his life would not have been worth living in Perth, where the people supported the Ruthvens. In the lack of additional witness, several tales spread about Henderson's departure from Perth during the day, as well as his presence in the kitchen during the crisis. He was last seen at the house right before the King's supper, and according to his version, the Master shut him up in the tower. Robertson's initial story was most likely accurate. Other witnesses denied seeing Gowrie's retainers, who were undoubtedly present during the quadrangle brawls to protect their neighbors. Henderson never explained why he bolted so quickly if he wasn't the guy on the turret. As a result, I believe that his tale is mostly genuine since he was at Falkland and returned early.

Given all of this, only one of two hypotheses is viable. The incident was not by chance; James did not panic and yell 'Treason!' out the window just because he found himself alone in a turret—and why in a remote turret?—with the Master. The gallery's closed door is an effective response to such an argument. Someone had it locked for some reason. As a result, either the Ruthvens conspired against the King or the King conspired against the Ruthvens. As we will see, both sides had fair reasons for hatred—that is, Gowrie and James had reasons to dispute; but with the young Master, whose cause, as concerns the lands of Scone, the King championed, he had no reason to be angry. How did James manage his fascination if he was guilty?

Let us imagine the King sets his scheme with reasons to despise Gowrie. He selects a day when he knows the Murrays of Tullibardine will be in Perth for one of the clan's weddings. They will protect the King against the townspeople, who are customers of their Provost, Gowrie.

James then invites Ruthven to Falkland (as Ruthven's defense claimed): he comes at the unusually early hour of 6.30 a.m. However, James has already concocted the pot of gold narrative to be said to Lennox as evidence that Ruthven is bringing him to Perth—that he has not invited Ruthven.

Next, by quietly disseminating rumors that he intends to seize the Master of Oliphant, James gets a large train of retainers, say twenty-five men without guns, while avoiding the suspicion that would be raised if he commanded them to follow him. Finally, James has decided to sacrifice Ruthven (with whom he has no beef) only as bait to lure Gowrie into a trap.

Having deceived Lennox into joining Ruthven alone in the mansion of Gowrie, James covertly prepares for Ruthven to discreetly ask him or Erskine to follow upstairs, intending to provoke Ruthven into a treasonable attitude just as they come on the scene. He predicts that Lennox, Erskine, or both would knife Ruthven without hesitation and that Gowrie would run forward to avenge his brother and be slaughtered.

His Majesty's well-planned scheme falls apart on the surface when Ruthven summons neither Lennox nor Erskine for reasons best known to himself. Observing this condition, James quickly and effectively remodels his strategy. He does not begin to cause the brawl until, for whatever reason, he is in the turret and hears his train conversing outside on the street. He had foreseen their appearance by instructing a servant of his own to propagate the false word of his departure, which Cranstoun had brought innocently. Why did the King do this, given that his initial plan did not need such a ruse? He had also convinced Gowrie to believe the tale despite the porter's rejection of its feasibility and stick with it while making no meaningful effort to confirm its veracity. Making Gowrie do this instead of carefully inspecting the home is undoubtedly the King's most spectacular and unexplained achievement.

As a result, the King has two strings to his malicious bow. The first was that Ruthven would fetch Erskine and Lennox on his instructions, and when they arrived, James would goad Ruthven into a treasonable attitude, after which Lennox and Erskine would dirk him. If this failed (which it did since Ruthven did not heed instructions), the second strategy was to trick Gowrie into bringing the retinue beneath the tower window, where the King could open the window and yell 'Treason!' as soon as he heard their voices and footfall below. This strategy is successful. James screams through the window. He had somehow sealed the entrance leading into the gallery while giving Ramsay a signal to wait outside the house, within earshot, and come up via the rear staircase constructed in a visible tower.

The rest is simple. Gowrie is free to bring up as many men as he wants. Still, Ramsay has been given orders to horrify him by claiming that the King has been slain (this was alleged) and then to run him through as he gives ground or drops his points; this after a decent form of resistance in which three of the King's four men are wounded.

'Master of the human heart,' like Lord Bateman, James understands that Ruthven will not just abandon him when provoked by insult and that Gowrie will not just stand in the street and call the townspeople when he learns of his brother's death.

To acquire a witness to the reality of his fraudulent account of events, James must have begun by ingeniously persuading Henderson, Gowrie's steward, either to flee and then return later with evidence or to be present in the turret and then flee. Perhaps the King uttered his man-in-the-turret story only 'in the air,' and Henderson, having fled in fright, later sees money in it,' and reappears with a series of lies. Aristotle says, 'Chance loves Art,' and chance may easily favor an artist as competent and moral as his Majesty. To be sure, Mr. Hill Burton claims that "the hypothesis that the entire thing was a Court plan to destabilize the mighty House of Gowrie must be discounted at immediately, after a calm weighing of the facts, as being outside the realm of logical conclusions." Those who formed it had to put one of the very last men in the world to accept such a fate in the position of an unarmed man who, without any preparation, was to render himself into the hands of his armed adversaries and cause a succession of surprises and acts of violence, which he would rule to a determined and preconcerted plan by his courage and skill.'

Without a strategy, James intended to start a quarrel and 'go it blind if there was a royal conspiracy.' This, however, goes much beyond the King's usual and amorous rashness. We must favor the notion of a finely coordinated and well-executed plan, built with alternatives so that if one thread breaks, another will hold tight. That strategy has been outlined to the best of my ability. To use an ironic phrase, everything of this notion is utterly unbelievable. James was not the kind of wildly daring individual who would go weaponless with Ruthven, who carried a sword and provoke him into arrogance. Even if he had been bold, the scheme is of such intricacy that no sane man, much alone a fearful guy, could concoct and carry out a scheme that is at the mercy of many unforeseeable variables. Assume the Master is dead, and Gowrie is a free man on the street. He merely had to sound the tocsin, gather his dedicated townspeople, surround the house, and gently request answers.

Take, for example, the hypothesis of Gowrie's guilt. The motivations for evil intent on either side may be simply outlined below. The Ruthvens had been the Crown's adversaries since the assassination of Riccio (1566). Gowrie's grandfather and father were leaders in the assault on Mary and Riccio; Gowrie's father humiliated Queen Mary by romantic attempts when imprisoned in Loch Leven Castle, she claims. In 1582, Gowrie's father kidnapped James and imprisoned him in deplorable conditions. He escaped and reunited with his jailer, who plotted again and was executed in 1584, while the Ruthven lands were forfeited. The Ruthvens were restored by a new revolution (1585-1586). In July 1593, Gowrie's mother, via a cunning ambush, allowed the Earl of Bothwell to abduct the King once again. Our Gowrie, being a youngster, joined Bothwell in open rebellion in 1594. He was pardoned and traveled abroad in August 1594, traveling as far as Rome, studying at Padua, and returning to England in March 1600, beckoned by the Kirk party. Elizabeth pampered him here, and he was then on practically warlike terms with James. For thirty years, Elizabeth had supported every treason of the Ruthvens, and Cecil had aided and abetted several attempts to seize James. As late as April 1600, these plots were plentiful. The goal was always to establish Kirk's supremacy over the King, and Gowrie, as the natural noble head of the Kirk, was summoned to Scotland in 1600 by the Rev. Mr. Bruce, the head of the political preachers whom James had controlled in 1596-97. When Gowrie arrived, he immediately took command of the Opposition and successfully opposed the King's request for supplies, which had been necessitated by his unfriendly ties with England, on June 21, 1600. Gowrie then left the Court and went hunting in Atholl about July 20, leaving his mother (who had previously enticed James into a trap) at his Perth home. On August 1, Gowrie informed his mother of his impending homecoming. She proceeded to the family stronghold of Dirleton, between North Berwick and the sea, while Gowrie arrived at his Perth home on August 3, with the understanding that he would ride to Dirleton on August 5. He had sent the majority of his soldiers and supplies there. We know he embarked on a longer adventure on August 5.

We've established that James' storyline is fantastic. Aside from the overall character of the events and the peculiar behavior of himself and his brother, there is no evidence to support a conspiracy by Gowrie. But, if he plotted, he was only carrying out the usual strategy of his grandparents, father, mother, and comrade, Bothwell, who was at the time in exile in Spain, ripening a conspiracy in which he claimed Gowrie as one of his confederates. Gowrie could not expect to rouse the disgruntled Barons or emancipate the preachers who had called him home while the King was still a free man. Instead, allow the King to flee, and Kirk's party, the English side, would prevail.

The implication is that the King was made to vanish, and Gowrie agreed to do so. Mr. Cowper, minister of Perth, and Mr. Rhynd, Gowrie's former teacher, testified that he was used to speaking of the necessity for absolute concealment 'in the accomplishment of a noble and perilous aim.' Such a goal as the capture of the King by a surprise onslaught was customary in Scottish politics. Cecil's records from this time and after that are replete with similar proposals presented by Scottish explorers. So it's no surprise that two guys as young as the Ruthvens would devise such a passionate and risky scheme.

Its initial intention must assess the scheme: to lure James to Perth at an early hour of the day with just two or three servants. If the King had visited Gowrie House early and sparsely attended, he might have been taken through Fife, disguised, in the procession of Gowrie as he traveled to Dirleton. From there, he might be transported by sea to Fastcastle, the impenetrable eyrie of Gowrie's and Bothwell's old friend, Logan of Restalrig. I have proven by comparison of handwritings that the famous letters considered by Scott, Tytler, and Hill-Burton as evidence of that conspiracy were all faked. Still, one of them, claimed by the forger as his model for the others, is, I believe, a fake copy of a real original. In that letter (to Gowrie), Logan is persuaded to compare their strategy to one devised against a "nobleman of Padua," where Gowrie had studied. This comment, in a postscript, cannot have been made up by the forger, Sprot, a low country attorney, and Logan's creation. The other letters are just variations on the melody established by this composition.

A scheme of this kind is not feasible, unlike the unbelievable conspiracy claimed to James. The concept was only one of several of its like that were continually being invented at the time. The next-to-impossible scenario is that Ruthven left Henderson, as he said, on the turret without tutoring in his role. The King's party did not think Henderson was telling the truth; he had accepted the role but turned cowardly, they said. This is especially plausible given that, in December 1600, a gentleman called Robert Oliphant, a servant of Gowrie, escaped from Edinburgh, where some admissions blabbed by him had gained public attention. He had claimed that Gowrie had persuaded him to play the armed man in the turret in Paris early in 1600; that he had 'with good cause dissuaded him; that the Earl after that left him and negotiated with Henderson in that matter; that Henderson attempted it and yet fainted'—that is, became craven. Though the Privy Council acquitted Oliphant of hiding treason nine years later in England, had he not departed from Edinburgh in December 1600, the whole case may have been made apparent since witnesses were then available.

We conclude that, because there was undoubtedly a Ruthven plot, and because the King could not have invented and carried out the affair, and because Gowrie, the leader of the Kirk party, was young, romantic, and 'Italianate,' he did plan a device of the regular and usual kind, but was frustrated, and fell into the pit which he had dug. Still, the Presbyterians would never accept that the youthful head of the Kirk party tried, and considerably more regularly plotted to do, what the godly leaders had often done, and considerably more often plotted to do, with Cecil and Elizabeth's full permission. The conspiracy was orthodox, but historians with Presbyterian and Liberal leanings assume that the King was the conspirator. The Ruthvens were long mourned, and women in Perthshire chanted to their babies, 'Sleep ye, sleep ye, my bonny Earl o' Gowrie,' even in the nineteenth century.

A woman has even written to tell me that she is a descendent of the younger Ruthven, who fled to England after being stabbed by Ramsay and Erskine, married, and had a family. I answered in vain that young Ruthven's corpse had been embalmed, shown in the Scottish Parliament, and chopped to bits, which were put on spikes in public locations, and that he was unlikely to marry after these ordeals. Nevertheless, the lady's faith was not to be shaken.

Mr. Edmund Gosse acknowledges Ramsay the Ruthven killer as the author of a Century of English Sonnets (1619), of which Lord Cobham holds an individual copy in The Atheneum for August 28, 1902. René Giffart published the book in Paris. Gifford's Scottish name was spelled 'Giffart,' indicating that the publisher was of Scottish heritage.

THE MYSTERY OF CAMPDEN

The average historical riddle is at least evident enough that one of two answers must be correct, if only we knew which. Perkin Warbeck was either the true King or an imposter. Giacomo Stuardo of Naples (1669) was Charles II's oldest son or charlatan. Mattioli or Eustache Dauger was undoubtedly the Man in the Iron Mask. Gowrie plotted against James VI., or James VI. plotted against Gowrie, and so on. These riddles are motivated by logic and human nature. But, save for one idea, there is no sparkle of reason or rational human nature at the heart of the Campden riddle. The happenings seem to be as random as those in a restless dream. 'The Whole Matter is dark and mysterious; which we must therefore leave to Him who alone knows all Things, in His rightful Time, to expose and bring to Light.'

According to the author of 'A True and Perfect Account of the Examination, Confession, Trial, and Execution of Joan Perry, and her two sons, John and Richard Perry, for the Supposed Murder of Will Harrison, Gent., Being One of the most extraordinary Occurrences that has transpired in the Memory of Man,' Sent in a letter to Thomas Shirly, Doctor of Physick, in London (by Sir Thomas Overbury, of Burton, in the County of Gloucester, Knt., and one of his Majesty's Justices of the Peace). Also, Mr. Harrison's account,' and so forth. (London: Printed for John Atkinson in St. Paul's Church-Yard, near the Chapter House. But, unfortunately, there is no date, although it seems to be 1676.)

Such is the wide and breathless title of a treatise that, by undeserved good fortune, has been published.

I'm lucky; I just bought it. Sir Thomas Overbury, 'the unfortunate victim of the evil Countess of Somerset' (who had the older Overbury poisoned in the Tower), was the Justice of the Peace who functioned as Juge d'Instruction in the case of Harrison's abduction, according to Mr. John Paget.

To get to the point of the narrative. At 1660, William Harrison, Gent., was steward or "factor" to the Viscountess Campden in Chipping Campden, Gloucestershire, a single-street village nestled in the Cotswold hills. The lady did not dwell at Campden House, which its owner burned down during the Great Rebellion to spite the rebels, much as its Jacobite ruler burned down castle Tirrim during the '15. Instead, Harrison lived in a section of the building that had not been destroyed. He had been a servant of the Hickeses and Campdens for fifty years, was seventy years old (which adds to the mystery), was married, and had children, including Edward, his oldest son.

Mr. Harrison's home was broken into at high noon on a market day in 1659, while he and his whole family were 'at the Lecture,' at church, a Puritan method of edifying. A ladder had been propped up against the wall, the bars of a second-story window had been yanked away with a plowshare (which had been left in the chamber), and 140 l. of Lady Campden's money had been taken. The thief was never apprehended, which is unusual in such a tiny and isolated community.

However, the times had changed, and a roaming Cavalier or Roundhead soldier may have 'cracked the crib.' Perry, Harrison's servant, was heard pleading for aid in the garden a few weeks later. He displayed a hacked-handled sheep-pick,' declaring that he had been attacked by two guys in white with bare swords and had defended himself with his primitive instrument. It is strange that Mr. John Paget, a sharp-witted writer who served as a police judge in Hammersmith for many years, mentions nothing about the heist of 1659 or Perry's insane behavior in the garden. Perry's actions there and his hysterical creation of the two armed guys in white reveal a lot about his personality. Of course, the two guys in white were never found, but we subsequently encounter three individuals who are no less obnoxious and much more strange. They seemed to be three men in buckram.'

In any case, even the unadventurous had experiences in peaceful Campden. They reached a climax the next year, on August 16, 1660. Harrison got up early (?) and traveled the two miles to Charringworth to collect his lady's rentals. The fall day was drawing in, and between eight and nine o'clock, old Mrs. Harrison sent her servant, John Perry, to meet his master on his way home. In Harrison's window, lights were also left on. That night, neither master nor man returned. It is curious that the younger Harrison, Edward, did not look for his father until very early the following morning: he had the advantage of a late-rising moon for nocturnal searching. In the morning, Edward saw Perry, returning alone: he had not located his master. The couple proceeded to Ebrington, a hamlet halfway between Campden and Charringworth, and discovered that Harrison had visited at the residence of one Daniel on the previous evening as he made his way home via Ebrington. The time is not specified, but Harrison vanished just past Ebrington, less than a mile from Campden. Next, Edward and Perry learned that a poor lady had found a hat, band, and comb belonging to Harrison on the route outside Ebrington, amid some whins or furze; they were discovered within approximately half a mile of his own home. The band was bloodied, and the cap and comb had been slashed and cut. Please take note of the exact words of Sir Thomas Overbury, the judge who presided over the preliminary examinations: 'The Hat and Comb were slashed and chopped, and the Band bloodied, but nothing more could be discovered.' As a result, the hat and comb were not on Harrison's head when they were chopped and chopped; otherwise, they would have been blood-stained; the band around the neck was bloody, but there was no evidence of blood on the road. This paragraph contains the solution to the riddle.

When word of the finding of these things spread, everyone raced to look for Harrison's body, which they did not locate.

An older man like Harrison was unlikely to remain at Charringworth very late, but whatever happened on the roadway seems to have occurred after nightfall.

Suspicion fell on John Perry, who was hauled before the narrator, Sir Thomas Overbury, J.P. Perry stated that on the previous evening, about 8.45 p.m., he started for

Charringworth to seek his master, and explained to him that because he was afraid in the dark, he would go back and take Edward Harrison's horse and return. Perry followed through on his promise, and Reed dropped him off 'at Mr. Harrison's Court gate.' Perry lingered there till one Pierce passed by, and with Pierce (for reasons unknown), 'he went a bow's shot into the fields,' and thus returned to Harrison's gate. He now rested for an hour in a hen-coop, woke at midnight, and set off towards Charringworth again; the moon had now risen and alleviated his concerns. However, he got lost in the mist, slept along the roadside, and then went to Charringworth in the morning, only to discover that Harrison had been there the day before. Then he returned and met Edward Harrison, who was on his way to find his father at Charringworth.

Perry's account seems like an idiot delivered it, but Reed, Pierce, and two guys from Charringworth verified it to the best of their abilities. Perry had certainly been in company with Reed and Pierce the night before, say between nine and ten o'clock. If anything bad had happened to Harrison, it had to have happened before ten o'clock at night; if he were sober, he would not have stayed that late at Charringworth. Was he always sober? His wife and son's calm demeanor during his absence implies that he was a late-wandering old lad. They could have anticipated Perry to find him in his drinks and put him into bed in Charringworth or Ebrington.

Perry was kept in jail or, more oddly, in the inn until August 24. He narrated numerous stories, such as how a tinker or a servant killed his master and concealed him in a bean-rick, where a search revealed no est inventus. Harrison, along with the rents he had collected, faded into the blue. Perry now claimed that he would only tell Overbury everything. Perry said that Harrison was slain by his mother and brother, Joan and Richard Perry! His brother had looted the home the previous year with John Perry's guidance and connivance, while John 'had a Halibi,' being at church. According to John, the money was buried in the garden by the brother. It was sought but not discovered. He said that his tale about the 'two guys in white' who had earlier assaulted him in the yard was fiction. I might emphasize that that was not a rational man's lie. Perry was insane.

He continued with his tales. His mother and brother, he said, had often requested that he informed them when his employer went to collect rent. He'd done so after Harrison set off for Charringworth on August 16th. Next, John Perry described his trip with his brother on the evening of the fateful day. This statement contradicted both his prior narrative of his actions and the legitimate testimony of Reed and Pierce. Their truthful version crushed Perry's latest lie. Next, he said that he and Richard Perry had followed Harrison into Lady Campden's grounds when he returned home at night; Harrison had used a key to the private gate. Richard followed him into the grounds; after a little walk, John Perry joined him there and discovered his mother (how did she get there?) and Richard standing over the prone Harrison, whom Richard incontinently murdered. They took Harrison's money and planned to bury him "in the vast sink at Wallington's Mill." John Perry had abandoned them and had no idea if the corpse had been put into the sink. In truth, neither the sink nor the bean-rick was invented. John then described his encounter with Pierce but completely forgot about his meeting with Reed and failed to account for that aspect of his initial tale, which Reed and Pierce had both supported. The hat, comb, and band that John said he had transported away from Harrison's corpse, cut with his knife and tossed into the roadway. He didn't disclose where the blood on the band originated from.

Joan and Richard Perry were arrested and hauled before Overbury based on this incomprehensible jumble of mad lies. The sink and the Campden fish-pools and the wrecked remains of the house were searched in vain for Harrison's remains. On August 25, Overbury interrogated the three Perrys, and Richard and the mother denied everything John charged them with. John persisted with his account, and Richard confirmed that he and John had talked on the morning of Harrison's disappearance, 'but nothing passed between them to that purpose.'

A tragic event occurred as the three were being transported from Overbury's residence to Campden. Richard, who was a long-distance behind John, slipped 'a ball of inkle from his pocket.' When one of his guards took it up, Richard explained that it was "only his wife's hair-lace." However, there was a slip-knot at one end. The finder handed it to John, who had not seen his brother drop it since he was so far ahead. When shown the thread, John shook his head and remarked, "To his sorrow, he recognized it, for it was the cord his brother strangled his master with." At the next trial, John swore in response to this event.

In September, the Assizes were conducted, and the Perrys were indicted for both the robbery in 1659 and the murder in 1660. They pled 'Guilty' to the first accusation, as someone in court advised them to do since the offense was covered by Charles II's Act of Pardon and Oblivion, which was enacted during his positive Restoration. If they were innocent of the robbery, as they most likely were, they made a mistake by pleading guilty. We hear of no proof against them for the heist, except John's confession, which was maybe evidence against John but not against them. They harmed their case since, if they were indeed responsible for the heist at Harrison's residence, they were the most probable individuals in the neighborhood to rob him again and kill him. They most likely used the excellent King's indemnification to tie the rope around their necks. They eventually recanted their testimony and were most likely innocent of the crime in 1659.

They were not tried in September on the murder accusation. Sir Christopher Turner refused to continue 'because Harrison's corpse had not been recovered.' There was no corpus delicti, no proof that Harrison had died. Meanwhile, John Perry said, as if to underscore his insanity, that his mother and brother had attempted to poison him in jail! Sir B. Hyde, who was less legal than Sir Christopher

Turner, tried the Perrys for murder at the Spring Assizes in 1661. How he could accomplish this is unclear since the narrative of the trial is not in the Record House, and I am unable to locate it at the moment. John Wesley published a narrative in the Arminian Magazine about a man executed for killing another man, whom he later encountered in one of South America's Spanish colonies. I won't interrupt the Perrys' story to explain how a hung guy met a murdered man. Still, the incident demonstrates that inflicting death punishment for murder without evidence of murder is unconstitutional and injudicious. It was probably expected that Harrison, if alive, would have shown indications of life within nine or ten months.

All three Perrys pleaded 'not guilty at the spring trial' with John's confession being used against him. 'He told them he was then angry and knew not what he said,' he claimed. So there has to be some proof against Richard. He said that his brother had implicated others in addition to himself. When pressed to provide proof, he said that "most of those who had testified against him knew it," but he did not identify any of them. So evidence had been presented (perhaps to the effect that Richard was loaded with cash), but we don't know who gave it or what effect.

The Perrys were most likely not well-known. Joan, the mother, was said to be a witch. This allegation was seldom leveled against well-to-do persons. The legends and records of trials in Glanvil's Sadducismus Triumphatus reveal how great the dread of witches was at the time. Joan Perry, as a witch, was likely to be 'nane the waur o' a hanging,' according to her neighbors. She was executed first, with the notion that her death would eliminate any hypnotic or other evil effects she had on her boys, preventing them from confessing. We are unaware that the suggester's death removes post-hypnotic suggestion; the experiment has not been conducted. Joan's experiment was a failure. Poor Richard, who was executed next, could not persuade the 'dogged and sullen' John to clear his name with a deathbed statement. Such utterances were formerly believed to be irrefutable proof, at least in Scotland, except where it did not suit the Presbyterians to believe the dying man (as in George Sprot, killed for the Gowrie plot). When John was cut off, he remarked, 'he knew nothing of his master's death, nor what had become of him, but they may afterward (perhaps) hear.' Was John privy to something? It wouldn't surprise me if he were aware of the true situation of the case.

They did hear, but what they heard, and what I'm about to tell you, was completely unbelievable. Will Harrison, Gent., like the three stupid ewes in the folk-rhyme, 'come hirpling hame' after some years (presumably two). What had happened to the older adult? In a letter to Sir Thomas Overbury, he explained in a letter, but his story is as implausible as John Perry's.

He claims to have left his home in the afternoon (rather than the morning) on Thursday, August 16, 1660. He went to

Charringworth to collect rents, but all of Lady Campden's tenants were harvesting. When you think about it, August seems like an unusual month for rent collection. They arrived home late, which caused Harrison to be late till the end of the evening. He only got 23 l., which John Perry said was paid by one Edward Plaisterer during his first examination in 1660, and Plasterer confirmed. Harrison then traveled home, most likely in the darkness, and towards Ebrington, where the road was narrow and surrounded with whins, 'there met me one horseman who asked "Art thou there?"' Afraid of being ridden over, Harrison punched the horse on the nose, and the rider struck at him and stabbed him in the side with a sword. (The cut hat and bloody band were discovered at this section of the road, where the whins grew, but a stab in the side would not make a neck-band bloody.) Two more riders arrived; one of them shot Harrison in the leg. They did not remove his 23 l., but instead put him behind one of them on horseback, shackled him, and draped a large robe over him.

Is it plausible that highwaymen would have handcuffs that closed with a spring and a snap, as Harrison suggests? The narrative is entirely fiction, and it's a lousy one at that. Suppose abduction, rather than robbery, was the motivation (which would explain the handcuffs). What could any mortal stand gain by kidnapping, for the intention of selling him into slavery, a 'gent.' of seventy years of age?

They grabbed Harrison's money and 'tumbled me into a stone pit in the middle of the night. After an hour, they hauled him out again, and he understandably inquired what they wanted with him, given that they already had his money. One of these thugs shot Harrison again and placed a large amount of money into his pockets. What did they want with 23 l. if they had a lot of money? We hear of no other robberies in the area from which the money may have been obtained. And why does Harrison have to carry the money? (It has been proposed that to gain public favor, they pretended to be smugglers, and Harrison, with the money, pretended to be their valiant purser, wounded in some heroic adventure.)

They traveled till late on August 17, when they dropped Harrison off at a lonely cottage, bleeding and sorely bruised with the transport of the money.' They served their victim broth and brandy here. They rode all day Saturday to a home where they stayed and then carried Harrison to Deal and placed him down on Sunday. It was about three o'clock in the afternoon. If they had wished to get to the sea, they would have naturally gone to the west shore. While one guy was watching Harrison, two others met a guy, and 'I overheard them say seven pounds.' As Harrison later learned, the guy who suggested seven pounds (Crenshaw later learned—where?) indicated he felt Harrison would die before being placed on a ship. What diable was he going to do in this galère? On the other hand, Harrison was sent on board a casual vessel and stayed on board for six weeks.

What was the location of the land to which the ship would sail?

Historical Mysteries

All the sailors know is how far ahead they are!

Harrison did not tell where the ship went roaming for six mortal weeks in the "foam of dangerous seas, amid faery realms lonely." Lord Bateman, for example:

He sailed eastward and westward.

Until he arrived in fabled Turkey.

Where he was apprehended and imprisoned

He was wear—ee! for the rest of his life!

'Then the Master of the ship arrived and informed me, and the other who was in the same predicament, that he detected three Turkish ships.' We're told that a full load of Harrisons was stolen and imprisoned aboard a ship released into the sea in the hopes that the captain would run across three Turkish rovers who would abduct them. At this pace, there must have been unexplained disappearances like Harrison's from dozens of English parishes in August 1660. If a crew of kidnappers had been capturing prisoners for personal fiscal reasons, they would have taken them to Virginian plantations, where Turkish galleys did not travel, and they would not have taken males over the age of seventy. Furthermore, kidnappers would not harm their hostages by stabbing them in the side and thigh if there was no resistance, as was done to Harrison.

'The remainder in the same condition' were 'dumped down' near Smyrna, where the precious Harrison was sold to a 'grave physician.'

This Turk was 87 years old and 'loved Crowland in Lincolnshire above all other areas in England.' Unfortunately, there are no recorded inquiries about a Turkish medical professional who previously practiced in Crowland, Lincolnshire, yet if he did, he was likely to be remembered in the area. Harrison used this Turk in the still room and as a laborer in the cotton fields, where he once knocked his slave down with his fist—pretty good for an eighty-seven-year-old Turk! He also gave Harrison (who worked in his company's chemical department) a "silver bowl, double gilt, to drink in, and dubbed him Boll"—his way of pronouncing bowl—no likely because he had acquired a Lincolnshire accent.

This Turk became sick on a Thursday and died the next Saturday when Harrison tramped to the closest port, bowl and all. Two sailors on a Hamburg ship denied him passage, but a third agreed to allow him on board for the price of his silver-gilt bowl. Harrison arrived in Lisbon without even his bowl when he met a guy from Wisbech, Lincolnshire. This kind Samaritan provided Harrison wine, strong waters, eight stivers, and transportation to Dover, from where he returned to Campden, much to the surprise of everyone. We don't know the identities of the ship or the captain that transported Harrison from Lisbon to Dover. The only person referenced in this dizzying tangle of insanity is Crenshaw (the guy seven pounds 'were mentioned').

'Many dispute the reality of this description Mr. Harrison

tells of himself, and his deportation, thinking he was never out of England,' writes the editor of our booklet. I'm not surprised by their skepticism. We are informed that Harrison had 'all his days been a man of sober life and discourse' and that he 'left behind him a significant amount of his Lady's money in his home.' On the night of his disappearance, he did not see any of the Perrys. The editor concedes that Harrison, as a commodity, was not worth the freight to Deal, much alone Smyrna. His son took over as Lady Campden's steward in his absence, and he acted horribly in that role. Some assumed that this son planned Harrison's capture, but if so, why did he secure John Perry's hanging, in chains, on Broadway hill, 'where he may daily view him'?

That might be a blind spot. But Harrison could not have expected John Perry to help him by implicating himself, his brother, and his mother, which was the most unexpected thing in the world. He had no idea that his father would return from Charringworth in the dark on August 16, 1660, and arrange for three riders armed with a great weight of money to stab and take off the aging patriarch. Young Harrison had not a big fardel of money to offer them, and since they were already so wealthy, what did they stand to gain by transporting Harrison to Deal and placing him on board a casual ship with "others in the same condition"? They might have left him in the stone-pit:' he had no idea who they were, and the longer they rode by daylight, with a hatless, shackled, and severely injured prisoner, his pockets bulging with money, the greater the chance of being discovered. So a group of three guys cycles across England in broad daylight, from Gloucestershire to Deal. Behind one of them lies a wounded, hatless, shackled victim with overflowing pockets. Nobody suspects anything, and no one alerts a judge to this great maneuver! It's much too ludicrous!

Harrison's narrative is obviously and childishly untrue. These strange horsemen must have been confronted at every baiting spot and inn. If Harrison were telling the truth, he would have identified the ship and captain that carried him to Dover.

After dismissing Harrison's tale, we wonder what may have caused his absence. On the evening of August 16, he strolled to within half a mile of his residence. He would not have done so if he had been intent on a senile amour involving his disappearance from home, and if that were his intention, he would have equipped himself with money. Again, a fit of 'ambulatory somnambulism,' with the formation of a split or dual personality and forgetting his true name and address, seems unlikely to have struck him at that precise time and location. If it occurred, he couldn't hurry out in a mob and travel discreetly across the countryside since there were no trains.

Again, the notion of ambulatory somnambulism fails to explain his chopped hat and bloodied band, which were discovered near the whins on the road beyond Ebrington. His narrative does not account for them either. He claims he was stabbed in the side and thigh. This would not result in the amputation of his headgear or the exsanguination of his band. On the other hand, he would leave pools and traces of blood on the road, dubbed "the highway." But there was nothing further discovered,' no pools or evidence of blood on the road. As a result, the cut hat and bloodied band were a deliberate false trail, not put there by John Perry, as he falsely claimed, but by someone else.

The implication is that Harrison's presence in Campden was inconvenient for someone. He had gone through the most trying moments and had found himself in a new situation with new rulers. He knew something about the turbulent times: he was a witness who should be kept out of the way. He may have kept a secret about one of the Regicides' cases or private interests since he was a loyal servant of a wealthy family. As a result, he was carried away, leaving an almost probably false trail—the cut hat and bleeding band. By a strange coincidence, his servant, John Perry, became insane—he was not rational on Thursday, August 16, and implicated himself, his brother, and his mother. During the two or three years that Harrison was missing, he was most likely never far from Campden. It was certainly made worthwhile for him to return and recount his crazy narrative, as well as accept the circumstance. There is no alternative explanation that 'collides the facts.' ' We'll never know what Harrison knew or why his absence was so important. But he was never a prisoner in 'famous Turkee.' 'It is hard to give a sufficient incentive for kidnapping the elderly man... considerable profit was not expected to result from the selling of the elderly man as a slave,' says Mr Paget. There was no profit, particularly given that the elderly guy was delivered in a damaged and damaged state. But finding a reason to keep Harrison out of the way is difficult since we don't know anything about his neighbours' private lives. Roundheads among them may have had compelling motives to keep Harrison imprisoned until the Restoration's vengeance were exacted. According to this perspective, the enigma virtually ceases to be strange since such insane self-accusations as John Perry's are not unusual.

CPSIA information can be obtained
at www.ICGtesting.com
Printed in the USA
LVHW011133230721
693494LV00003B/417